W9-BYH-544

WORLD HISTORY

Genghis Khan and the Mongol Empire

By Don Nardo

LUCENT BOOKS
A part of Gale, Cengage Learning

GALE
CENGAGE Learning™

Detroit • New York • San Francisco • New Haven, Conn • Waterville, Maine • London

LIBRARY OF CONGRESS CATALOGING-IN-PUBLICATION DATA

Nardo, Don, 1947-
  Genghis Khan and the Mongol Empire / by Don Nardo.
    p. cm. -- (World history)
  Includes bibliographical references and index.
  ISBN 978-1-4205-0326-5 (hardcover)
  1. Genghis Khan, 1162-1227--Juvenile literature. 2. Mongols--Kings and rulers--Biography--Juvenile literature. 3. Mongols--History--Juvenile literature. I. Title.
  DS22.N36 2010
  950'.21092--dc22

                                                        2010032960

Lucent Books
27500 Drake Rd.
Farmington Hills, MI 48331

ISBN-13: 978-1-4205-0326-5
ISBN-10: 1-4205-0326-X

Printed in the United States of America
1 2 3 4 5 6 7 14 13 12 11 10

Printed by Bang Printing, Brainerd, MN, 1st Ptg., 11/2010

Contents

Foreword   4
Important Dates at the Time of
Genghis Khan and the Mongol Empire   6

Introduction
From Barbarian to Modern Man   8

Chapter One
Ancient Peoples of the Steppes   14

Chapter Two
The Rise of Genghis Khan   27

Chapter Three
Military and Legal Reforms   39

Chapter Four
Subduing Northern China   52

Chapter Five
Conquests in Western Asia   65

Chapter Six
The Mongols After Genghis Khan   75

Notes   84
Glossary   87
For More Information   89
Index   91
Picture Credits   95
About the Author   96

Foreword

Each year, on the first day of school, nearly every history teacher faces the task of explaining why his or her students should study history. Many reasons have been given. One is that lessons exist in the past from which contemporary society can benefit and learn. Another is that exploration of the past allows us to see the origins of our customs, ideas, and institutions. Concepts such as democracy, ethnic conflict, or even things as trivial as fashion or mores, have historical roots.

Reasons such as these impress few students, however. If anything, these explanations seem remote and dull to young minds. Yet history is anything but dull. And therein lies what is perhaps the most compelling reason for studying history: History is filled with great stories. The classic themes of literature and drama—love and sacrifice, hatred and revenge, injustice and betrayal, adversity and overcoming adversity – fill the pages of history books, feeding the imagination as well as any of the great works of fiction do.

The story of the Children's Crusade, for example, is one of the most tragic in history. In 1212 Crusader fever hit Europe. A call went out to the pope that all good Christians should journey to Jerusalem to drive out the hated Muslims and return the city to Christian control. Heeding the call, thousands of children made the journey. Parents bravely allowed many children to go, and entire communities were inspired by the faith of these small Crusaders. Unfortunately, many boarded ships captained by slave traders, who enthusiastically sold the children into slavery as soon as they arrived at their destination. Thousands died from disease, exposure, and starvation on the long march across Europe to the Mediterranean Sea. Others perished at sea.

Another story, from a modern and more familiar place, offers a soul-wrenching view of personal humiliation but also the ability to rise above it. Hatsuye Egami was one of 110,000 Japanese Americans sent to internment camps during World War II. "Since yesterday we Japanese have ceased to be human beings," he wrote in his diary. "We are numbers. We are no longer Egamis, but the number 23324. A tag with that number is on every trunk, suitcase and bag. Tags, also, on our breasts." Despite such dehumanizing treatment, most internees worked hard to control their bitterness. They created workable communities inside the camps and demonstrated again and again their loyalty as Americans.

These are but two of the many stories from history that can be found in the pages of the Lucent Books World History series. All World History titles rely on sound research and verifiable evidence, and all give students a clear sense of time, place, and chronology through maps and time-lines as well as text.

All titles include a wide range of authoritative perspectives that demonstrate the complexity of historical interpretation and sharpen the reader's critical thinking skills. Formally documented quotations and annotated bibliographies enable students to locate and evaluate sources, often instantaneously via the Internet, and serve as valuable tools for further research and debate.

Finally, Lucent's World History titles present rousing good stories, featuring vivid primary source quotations drawn from unique, sometimes obscure sources such as diaries, public records, and contemporary chronicles. In this way, the voices of participants and witnesses as well as important biographers and historians bring the study of history to life. As we are caught up in the lives of others, we are reminded that we too are characters in the ongoing human saga, and we are better prepared for our own roles.

ca. 1162
Temujin, the future
Genghis Khan, is
born in Mongolia.

1215
In England King John
signs the Magna Carta.

1223
The Franciscan order
of monks is founded
in Europe.

ca. 1178
Temujin marries
Borte, a young
woman from a
different tribe.

1204
Temujin defeats
Jamuka, an old friend
turned enemy, in battle.

1227
Genghis Khan dies.

1162	1172	1182	1192	1202	1212	1222	1232	1242

1187
In Palestine a Muslim
army attacks the
Latin kingdom of
Jerusalem.

1219
The Mongols, led
by Genghis Khan,
invade Persia.

1230
In Africa the
Kingdom of
Mali gives
way to the
empire of
Ghana.

1169
Italy's Mount Etna volcano
erupts, killing an estimated
fifteen thousand people.

1206
The Mongols proclaim
Temujin Genghis
Khan, meaning
"Universal Leader."

1206–1218
Genghis Khan issues his
new code of laws and
justice, the Great Yasa.

1241
A Mongol army
defeats a coalition of
eastern Europeans at
Liegnitz, in Poland.

Genghis Khan and the Mongol Empire

1264
Another of Genghis Khan's grandsons, Kublai, takes charge of the Mongol Empire.

1251
Genghis Khan's grandson, Mongke, becomes Great Khan.

1294
Kublai Khan dies and no Great Khan takes his place.

| 1252 | 1262 | 1272 | 1282 | 1292 | 1302 | 1312 | 1322 | 1332 |

1256
The Hanseatic League is established in Scandinavia.

1281
Kublai launches an unsuccessful attempt to invade Japan.

1325
In Mexico the Aztecs establish their capital city of Tenochtitlán.

1265
The institution of Parliament emerges in England.

From Barbarian to Modern Man

In the thirteenth century, Mongolia, the region of eastern Asia lying north of China, became the launching point for a series of events that shocked and forever changed the world. Under their leader, who came to be known as Genghis Khan, Mongol armies pushed outward from their ancestral homeland. Like an unstoppable wave, they swept across the continent, destroying or seizing control of city after city and nation after nation. China fell to them. So did central Asia and much of the Middle East. And eventually, led by the Khan's successors, the fearsome invaders attacked Japan in the east and Europe in the west. In the span of a mere two centuries, hundreds of thousands of people died and tens of millions were conquered or displaced.

Partly for these reasons, later generations developed an extremely unflattering image of the Mongols. Even well into the twentieth century, most saw them as a primitive, barbaric people who raped and pillaged without mercy. In this view, they and their most famous leader, Genghis Khan, demolished everything in their path without a thought for preserving the fruits of civilization.

Both Good and Bad Qualities

Although this ugly portrait of the Mongols does contain some grains of truth, more recent studies have shown that it is also exaggerated and misleading in a number of ways. In particular, modern scholars have significantly reevaluated and refurbished the image of Genghis Khan. They do not dispute that he was a ruthless conqueror responsible for the deaths of thousands of innocent people. Yet, some of these experts point out, so were a number of larger-than-life Western military leaders, including Greece's Alexander the Great and France's Napoléon Bonaparte. And no one calls Alexander

A map of the Mongol Empire in the thirteenth century, which was carved out under the leadership of Genghis Khan.

or Napoléon a barbarian. Rather, such leaders are usually described as having both bad and good qualities, with some of the good ones canceling out, or at least balancing, the bad ones. Alexander, for instance, was undoubtedly an arrogant and cold-blooded dictator. Yet he also built dozens of new cities and fostered cultural exchanges, trade, and intermarriage between Greeks and the peoples he conquered.

Similarly, the reevaluations of Genghis Khan reveal him as a sometimes callous and cruel leader who also possessed certain positive qualities. Granted, he was not as noble and lofty as the renowned

English writer Geoffrey Chaucer made him out to be. In his poem *The Canterbury Tales*, penned in about 1380, Chaucer presents a highly romanticized version of the Mongol leader, whom he calls Cambinskan. Chaucer writes,

> There was nowhere in the wide world known
> So excellent a lord in everything;
> He lacked in naught belonging to a king.
> As for the faith to which he had been born,
> He kept its law to which he had been sworn;

A map of Mongolia as it exists today.

And therewith he was hardy, rich, and wise . . .
[And] in warfare ambitious
As any bachelor knight of all his house.
Of handsome person, he was fortunate,
And kept always so well his royal state
That there was nowhere such another man.[1]

Although Genghis Khan was not the idealized European monarch pictured by Chaucer, the writer correctly drew a portrait of a great ruler rather than of a pitiless, thoughtless savage. Indeed, a reading of the available evidence shows the famous Mongol to be a leader of amazing talent, versatility, and at times wisdom. Further, these qualities did not emerge solely on the battlefield, where he frequently showed brilliance. He also demonstrated highly effective political skills and vision, created a strict but fair law code, and championed religious freedom for all.

Moreover, no great or wise ruler or thinker taught Genghis Khan these skills and abilities. They came to him—the product of a poverty-stricken upbringing on the edge of the civilized world—quite naturally. Along with the awe he inspired in millions of people, such abilities allowed him to achieve remarkable deeds, including carving out the largest land empire in human history. One of his chief modern biographers writes,

> In American terms, the accomplishment of Genghis Khan might be understood if the United States, instead of being created by a group of educated merchants or wealthy planters, had been founded by one of its illiterate slaves, who, by the sheer force of personality, charisma, and determination, liberated America from foreign rule, united the people, created an alphabet, wrote the constitution, established universal religious freedom, invented a new system of warfare, marched an army from Canada to Brazil, and opened roads of commerce in a free-trade zone that stretched across the continents. On every level … the scope of Genghis Khan's accomplishments challenges the limits of imagination and taxes the resources of scholarly explanation.[2]

Deciphering the Mongols' Secrets

It is only natural to ask why the Mongols and their greatest leader, Genghis Khan, were so thoroughly reevaluated in recent times. Why did their image as monstrous barbarians with no redeeming qualities give way to one of aggressive

An ink portrait depicts Mongol ruler Genghis Khan.

conquerors who balanced their warlike acts with numerous constructive policies and achievements? To be sure, for a long time peoples throughout Asia, the Middle East, and Europe routinely blamed the Mongol "destroyers" for their own shortcomings. Soviet Russian leaders in the early twentieth century are a good example. When Russia fell behind Britain, the United States, and other Western countries in developing modern technologies, leaders claimed it was largely because of devastation wrought on Russia by the Mongols centuries before. Similarly, Chinese, Indian, and Arab leaders all cited centuries of Mongol brutality and oppression as a reason that they, too, were less technologically and militarily advanced than the West. Later, both the repressive Taliban regime in Afghanistan and Iraqi dictator Saddam Hussein complained about the long-ago Mongol invasions of their lands; they also compared the intervention of U.S. troops in their countries between 1991 and 2003 to the those medieval invasions.

Such arguments no longer carry much weight for two main reasons. First, some reliable old literary works that recorded the Mongols' constructive deeds, as well as their destructive ones, surfaced in the twentieth century. The most important is a work titled *The Secret History of the Mongols*. It is called "secret" because it was extremely difficult to decipher and for a long time remained mysterious. Although written in Chinese characters, each character stood for a sound in the Mongolian language of the thirteenth century. When the work was finally decoded and translated in the 1980s, it was clear that it had been composed by an anonymous Mongol author in the years immediately following Genghis Khan's death in the early thirteenth century. Thus, the writer had witnessed at least some of the recent Mongol conquests firsthand. Although the text contains elements of folklore and is sometimes inconsistent, it also includes a wealth of factual and reliable information about Genghis Khan's life and exploits and about Mongol culture in that era.

One way that modern scholars can tell what is or is not reliable in the *Secret History* is to compare its statements and claims to those in other existing histories from other Asian lands and peoples. Another way is to conduct archaeological digs in Mongolia and surrounding regions. Tombs, houses, weapons, human remains, and other artifacts can often verify if a claim made in a literary source is true or suspect.

The Tingling of a Bell

Such studies and artifacts are the second main reason that Genghis Khan and the Mongols were reevaluated in recent years. In 1990 the Soviet Union, ruled by a repressive Communist regime, collapsed. And Mongolia, which had long been under Soviet rule and cut off from the outside world, was suddenly free. Scholars from the United States and other Western nations hurried into that country and for the first time in the modern era began studying the Mongolians, their culture, and their historical sites and heritage up close. This research, which is still ongoing, has produced a large amount of valuable information about the Mongol Empire and its creation by Genghis Khan. "Gradually," recalls one of the researchers, anthropologist Jack Weatherford, "we pieced together the story [of Genghis Khan] as best we could with the evidence we had. By finding the places of [his] childhood, and retracing the path of events across the land, some misconceptions regarding his life could be immediately corrected."[3]

In these ways, a truer and more-balanced view of the great Mongol leader's deeds, both destructive and constructive, has emerged. In the words of distinguished University of London scholar George Lane, "Beneath the rhetoric and propaganda, behind the battles and massacres, hidden by the often self-generated myths and legends, the reality of the two centuries of Mongol ascendancy was often one of regeneration, creativity, and growth."[4] This new picture of Genghis Khan reveals that, although he invaded nations and slaughtered many of their inhabitants, he also remade them and set them on new historical paths, some of which eventually led them into the turbulent political and economic currents of the modern world. As Weatherford points out,

Although he arose out of the ancient tribal past, Genghis Khan shaped the modern world of commerce, communication, and large secular [nonreligious] states more than any other individual. He was the thoroughly modern man in his mobilized and professional warfare and his commitment to global commerce and the rule of international secular law. ... Like the tingling vibrations of a bell that we can still sense well after it has stopped ringing, Genghis Khan has long passed from the scene, but his influence continues to reverberate through our time.[5]

Chapter One

Ancient Peoples of the Steppes

The renowned Mongol leader Genghis Khan and the people he ruled arose from one of the world's most visually striking but also harshest environments. The setting for their highly distinctive culture was north-central Asia's vast expanse of steppes, or grass-covered, windswept plains. Most of what is now Mongolia, situated north of China, encompasses such steppes. And their singular high-altitude terrain and climate consistently challenged and tested the ancient peoples who inhabited them, among them the group that history came to call the Mongols.

A major reason that these peoples led a difficult existence is that the region was (and is) subject to marked extremes of temperature and precipitation. As scholar J.J. Saunders describes it,

> From June to August the steppe is a green carpet of grass and flowers, whose growth is promoted by heavy rains. In September the cold is already severe, in October snowstorms sweep across the land, by November the [rivers and other] water courses are frozen, and until the following May snowfalls are frequent and winds blow with such ferocity as almost to lift a rider from his saddle. The height and rarified atmosphere sometimes induce giddiness and exhaustion, and the lack of oxygen often obliges the nomad to desist from his attempts to kindle a fire. The monotony [boredom] of the steppe is notorious. As far as the eye can travel, it sees little but a flat wilderness, broken by occasional ravines and stony hills where no tree is visible.[6]

Beyond these vast, unforgiving plains rise high, craggy mountain ranges. In the foothills one finds willows and poplars near the streams; they bloom only briefly,

The high-altitude terrain and harsh climate of what is now known as Mongolia constantly challenged the ancient peoples who inhabited the area.

however, in the short summers. Farther up, cedars, pines, and larches grow, but are snow covered for much of the year, making travel along the slopes very difficult and in some places impossible.

Nomads and Pastoral Armies

In the midst of this tough, demanding, and sometimes-cruel setting dwelled a long succession of ancient peoples. Archaeologists have determined that the region was inhabited one hundred thousand years ago and likely considerably earlier. The initial residents were hunter-gatherers who followed herds of deer, horses, and other large mammals and lived off the land. Over

time they learned to domesticate some of their prey, including horses and cattle. That gave them an easier-to-acquire, more-stable food supply.

In fact, raising livestock was the steppe peoples' main way of making a living. They sustained themselves by consuming milk and other dairy products (and to a lesser degree meat), made their clothes from wool and hides, and used animal manure as fuel for fires. To maintain a constant supply of such items, they needed to move from place to place on a seasonal basis to find fertile pastures for their animals. And when they traveled, they packed up all they owned and set up a new temporary camp in the next pasture. This lack of a fixed place to live

Two fighting warriors depict the double role a pastoral nomad was required to play: one of herdsman as well as that of fighter and raider.

made them nomadic, which meant that they had no towns or other permanent settlements. Furthermore the temporary camps and livestock had to be guarded against attack by neighboring groups, which required that all members of society learn to fight at an early age. Scholar George Lane writes,

Constantly on the move, constantly alert to the environmental, climatic, and human changes around them, and constantly prepared for danger and threats, the pastoral nomads were a natural martial [warlike] force, and war was everyone's business. Every herdsman doubled as a fighter and raider, and the culture of the steppe resounded with tales and songs of their warrior heroes. These nomads were pastoral armies.[7]

Archaeology also reveals that by roughly 1000 B.C. the inhabitants of the region had learned to make tools and weapons from bronze, an alloy of copper and tin. This made activities such as hunting, slaughtering animals, and fighting more efficient. That efficiency increased even more when the people gained knowledge of iron making around 300 B.C. Iron implements were harder and more durable than those made of bronze.

The nomadic peoples who lived on the steppes north and west of China in 300 B.C. and the centuries that followed had developed more than improved metal technology. They had also forged strong individual group identities. And one group often opposed and fought one or more neighboring groups. Although the physical cultures and habits of all the groups were quite similar, they differed in certain basic ways, a major one being language. Some spoke variations of a basic ancient tongue that modern experts call Turkic. Ancient Asian steppe peoples who spoke forms of Turkic included the Tatars (also known as Tartars), Xiongnu, Uyghurs, Bulgars, and Huns. A second major language group of the region, proto-Mongolic, was spoken by groups including the Donghu, Ruruan (or Juan-Juan), Kitan, and Menggu (or Mongols).

Between 300 B.C. and A.D. 1200 these and a few other related groups of steppe nomads periodically fought one another. But an even more frequent enemy for many of them was the Chinese. China had long before developed a more organized and technically advanced civilization. It featured large-scale agriculture; permanent settlements, including numerous towns and cities; and much accumulated wealth, including precious metals like gold.

Seeking to acquire some of this wealth, group after group of steppe peoples raided northern China, with varying degrees of success. Beginning in the 200s B.C., for example, the Xiongnu attacked the Chinese repeatedly for more than two centuries. The Ruruan, who appear to be the first Mongolic speakers to use the term *khan*, meaning "overall leader," created a nomadic empire and raided Chinese towns in the 400s and 500s A.D. By 925 the Kitan were in control of eastern Mongolia and northern China. The two and a half centuries that followed witnessed frequent strife between the Kitan, Tatars, Menggu, and other groups in Mongolia. It was from the midst of this rivalry and dissension that Genghis Khan eventually arose and imposed unity on the region's peoples.

The Tribe and Family

One of the crucial and most difficult realities that Genghis Khan had to contend with was that the Mongol peoples were fiercely tribal as well as nomadic. Indeed, the basic unit of Mongol society was the tribe, or *irgen*. A typical tribe was a group of several hundred or maybe a few thousand people related by blood. They traveled and lived together in a close-knit unit overseen by a few elders, one of whom served as chief, or *gurkhan*. Lane explains that such a tribe

promoted unity and the idea of a common identity. [All] members of the tribe ... considered themselves descendants of a common ancestry, however tenuous and mythical that ancestry might be. ... Fiercely independent, there was little social cohesion above the level of the tribe, and tribal leaders generally resisted the formation of [higher] authority unless the forfeiting of their autonomy [independence] promised very great rewards.[8]

In terms of organization and family ties, a Mongol tribe typically broke down into several clans. A clan, or *obok*, was a kinship group composed of two to seven families. The clan head, called a *batur*, led the clan's fighters in battle. In contrast, during peacetime, the *batur* usually deferred to the heads of individual families. Family heads were always men because the nomadic steppe societies were patriarchal, or male dominated.

Being the head of a Mongol family was no easy task because the average family was quite large by modern standards. Some men had two or more wives and each wife usually produced several children. Also, grandparents, aunts, uncles, in-laws, and cousins were also viewed as members of a family.

The Hunt for a Bride

In his book, *Daily Life in the Mongol Empire*, George Lane, a noted expert on the Mongols, describes some singular customs involved in Mongol marriage:

When a marriage contract was drawn up, it was the father [of the bride] who organized the banquet. Meanwhile, the daughter was obliged to flee and hide from her future husband at the home of her relatives. The father would then announce the disappearance of his daughter and would tell her fiancé that if he could find her he could keep her. At this, the man would ride out with his friends to hunt for his betrothed. Upon finding her, he was supposed to feign [pretend] violence and forcibly seize her. ... As their daughter was being abducted, her family would be at home mourning their loss while the husband's family would be preparing a welcoming feast to greet his newly won wife.

George Lane, *Daily Life in the Mongol Empire*, Westport, CT: Greenwood, 2006, pp. 27–28.

Not surprisingly, the largest families could not fit comfortably in a single dwelling, which was typically small. So it was fairly common for the members of one family to live in two or more houses, which stood together in a compact cluster.

Building and Moving Homes

In both materials and looks, Mongol houses were very different from the majority of those in modern countries like the United States. Because the Mongols were nomads, who moved frequently from place to place, their dwellings had to be easily moveable. Moreover, they had to utilize building materials that were readily available on the steppes and in the mountains bordering them. Two of the most common materials were wool, derived from indigenous sheep and camels, and wood, from the trees that grew in the hills. An average Mongol house, called a *ger* (and later a yurt), was a sort of tent, or lodge, made from a wooden frame with layers of compressed wool, or felt, stretched across it. Because heavy rains could occur with little warning, the felt needed to be waterproof. To accomplish this, builders coated it with animal fat, still another product that came from their herds of livestock. In addition, according to a European monk

A yurt—an average Mongol house like the one pictured—was made from wood and layers of wool. The dwellings had to be easily moveable because of the Mongols' nomadic nature.

Ancient Peoples of the Steppes ■ 19

While smaller homes were taken apart to be moved, many of the Mongols' larger more elaborate homes required oversized carts so they could be moved intact.

named William of Rubruck, who visited Mongolia in the thirteenth century, it was common to smear

the felt with chalk, or white clay, or powdered bone, to make it appear whiter and sometimes they also make the felt black. The felt around [the] top [of the tent] they decorate with various pretty designs. Before the entry [door], they suspend felt ornamented with various embroidered designs in color. For they embroider the felt … making [pictures of] vines and trees, and birds, and beasts.[9]

Such a steppe dwelling was most often about 16 feet (5m) across, although smaller and larger versions existed. Inside, family members constructed a floor made of wooden planks covered by wool mats. In the center of the lodge they erected a stone hearth in which the family burned dung patties or wood for cooking and heating. The smoke vented to the outside through a hole at the top of the dwelling.

Moving such temporary but often elaborate homes was a major operation that involved all of a tribe's residents and many of their animals. The smaller, less-complex lodges were taken apart

How Koumiss Was Made

William of Rubruck, a European monk, visited Mongolia in the thirteenth century and watched the making of a Mongol drink called koumiss (also spelled kumiss).

They stretch a long rope on the ground fixed to two stakes stuck in the ground, and to this rope they tie toward the third hour the colts of the mares they want to milk. … When they have got together a great quantity of milk, which is as sweet as cow's as long as it is fresh, they pour it into a big skin or bottle, and they set to churning it with a stick prepared for that purpose … and when they have beaten it sharply it begins to boil up like new wine and to sour or ferment, and they continue to churn it until they have extracted the butter. Then they taste it, and when it is mildly pungent, they drink it. It is pungent on the tongue [when] drunk, and when a man has finished drinking, it leaves a taste of milk of almonds on the tongue, and it makes the inner man most joyful and also intoxicates weak heads, and greatly provokes urine.

Quoted in William W. Rockhill, ed. and trans., *The Journey of William of Rubruck to the Eastern Parts of the World, 1953–55*, London: Hakluyt Society, 1900, p. 19. http://depts.washington.edu/silkroad/texts/rubruck.html#kumiss.

and loaded onto wooden carts drawn by oxen or horses. They were then relatively quickly reconstructed at the next campsite. Some of the more sturdy and ornamented homes were actually loaded intact onto specially built oversize carts. William of Rubruck recalled that he saw one house measuring 30 feet (9m) wide placed on an enormous cart that required twenty-two oxen to pull. "The axle of the cart was as large as the mast of a ship," he said, "and one man stood in the entry of the house on the cart driving the oxen."[10]

Clothing and Food

The carts also carried the tribe's clothing and other personal belongings, as well as food. Men and women alike wore pants made of wool over which hung a tunic or robe-like outer garment of wool or leather. Women's tunics were somewhat longer and sometimes more decorated than men's. In colder weather both men and women lined their tunics with wool or fur and if necessary donned extra capes and/or fur hoods. They also wore leather boots, lined with fur in the winter, and hats fashioned of fur or other materials.

Both Mongol men and women wore a wool or leather tunic draped over wool pants.

They eat so little meat that other peoples could scarcely live from it. And further, they eat all kinds of meats except for that of the mule, which is sterile, and this they do disgracefully and rapaciously [greedily]. They lick their greasy fingers and wipe them dry on their boots. [And] they do not wash their hands before eating, nor their dishes afterwards.[11]

When the Mongols did eat animals, they tried not to waste any part of the beasts. They chewed and sucked the marrow from the bones, and they saved extra bones to gnaw on later in a leather bag called a *captargac*. They also used other parts of the animals to make clothes, housing, and other everyday items.

The Importance of Horses

When times were good, foodstuffs were abundant enough to keep a tribe well supplied. But when drought or other natural setbacks occurred, the Mongols ate what they had to in order to survive, for as one scholar puts it, survival was "an imperative [crucial need] overriding all generosity, all squeamishness." When necessary, he says, the Mongols

As was the case with clothes, the foods the members of the tribe ate came mainly from their domesticated animals, including sheep, goats, and cattle. One of their staple foods, for instance, was koumiss, a white alcoholic drink made from horse's milk. Milk from horses, cows, and other animals was also used to make a variety of cheeses. Tribal members also gathered wild grains, which they boiled to make an oatmeal-like porridge.

The Mongols did eat meat, although not very often because they slaughtered their animals only when they felt it was necessary. A Dominican friar and diplomat named Simon de Saint Quentin, who traveled through Asia in the 1240s, describes meat eating, along with table manners, among the Mongols:

would eat mice, dead animals found beside the trail, even their own dogs or cats when times were hard enough. And times often were. If a man found himself alone and desperate … he would open one of his horse's veins and drink the blood, but would make sure he sealed the wound when he had finished, for

Mongols learned to ride horses at an early age. The Mongols and other nomadic peoples relied on horses to travel and fight effectively in battle.

his horse was his key to success on the steppe.[12]

Indeed, horses, the healthier and stronger the better, were vital assets to the Mongols and other nomadic peoples of the steppes. In the narrative of the *Secret History*, a young Mongol man remarks, "If my horse dies, then I'll die. If my horse lives, then I'll live."[13] This was no exaggeration. Without these animals, one could not travel far or fight effectively in battle. Therefore, young Mongols learned to ride horses at an early age. Such a horse, scholar Peter Brent writes,

was no more than pony-sized, [but] deep-chested [and] heavily boned and muscled. Frequently evil-tempered, it was of an endless courage, able to subsist summer and winter on what it wrenched from the often inhospitable earth. It offered him the freedom of his world. As a result, Mongol and horse became a single, centaur-like entity. Babies rode before they could stand. When they grew up, sitting in the saddle was probably more natural to them than walking. While riding, Mongols ate, slept, drank, argued, and fought. As a result, horses became a symbol of prestige, marking out ... the rich and powerful. Conversely, stealing them was among the most heinous crimes a Mongol could commit.[14]

Mongol Women

Even though horses fulfilled certain essential tasks and needs in Mongol society, a great deal of the tribes' work was performed by women. First, women did all of the food preparation and cooking. They also bore and cared for the children, made the clothes, did periodic repairs on the family dwellings, and dismantled and loaded the dwellings onto carts when it was time to move to a new campsite. (Men, meanwhile, constructed the carts, hunted, made weapons and saddles, and fought the tribe's battles.)

In addition to her regular tasks, a young Mongol woman was expected to get married. She rarely, if ever, had any

Mongol women did a great deal of the tribe's work: cooking, making clothes, caring for the children, and dismantling and loading the tribe's dwellings into carts.

say in who her husband was, however. The Mongols and most other steppe peoples practiced exogamy, or marrying someone outside one's native tribe. Such marriages between tribes were arranged by tribal elders. Most commonly, the young man's father met with the young woman's father and agreed on the time and place of the marriage ceremony. Occasionally, though, young men were known to buy or even steal young women from rival tribes. If, over time, a man acquired multiple wives, he usually selected a favorite and paid more attention to her than to the other wives.

Mongol women were far from helpless and docile, however. They were able to ride horses and shoot bows as well as men, and if their camp was ambushed, they fought right beside their husbands, fathers, and brothers. In a document titled *Story of the Mongols*, a thirteenth-century Italian monk named Giovanni Carpini describes the wide range of skills, including military ones, that Mongol women possessed:

The girls and women gallop on their horses just as skillfully as the men. We also saw them carrying bows and quivers. Both men and women can stay in the saddle for a long time. ... All work rests on the shoulders of the women. They make fur coats, clothes, shoes [and] everything else made from leather. They also drive the carts and mend them, load the [pack animals], and are very quick and efficient in all their work. All women wear trousers, and some of them shoot with the bow as accurately as the men.[15]

Religious Beliefs

In addition to being nomadic, warlike, and socially patriarchal, the Mongols, like other ancient and medieval peoples, were spiritual. Compared to Christians, Jews, Muslims, and Buddhists, however, with whom the tribes of the steppes eventually came into contact, the Mongols were much less formal and organized in their faith. They had no official sacred writings, like the Bible or the Koran, for example, or written moral teachings like the ones in those books. Nor did the Mongols believe in a single, all-powerful god or have formal, permanent buildings for worship, like churches or mosques.

Rather, the original Mongol religion was a form of shamanism. It held that large numbers of invisible spirits existed, some inhabiting natural objects like trees and hills and others consisting of deceased Mongol ancestors. The most powerful spirit of all, the Mongols believed, was Tengri (or Tenggeri). His name means "Eternal Blue Sky," reflecting that people thought he dwelled somewhere in the sky. Another

Cleansing Mongol Sins

The medieval Italian monk Giovanni Carpini wrote about the concepts of sin and its purification in the traditional Mongol religion. Because the Mongols thought that a nature spirit dwelled in fire, he said, it was a sin to pass a knife through a campfire's flames. Similarly "it is a sin to lean on the whip with which they beat horses ... to touch arrows with the whip, to catch or kill young birds ... to break one bone with the help of another ... or to urinate inside a tent." Carpini also explained that the Mongols used fire to purify certain sins. When a person died, for instance, his or her belongings were carried between two fires, thereby, it was thought, cleansing them of evil.

Giovanni Carpini, *The Story of the Mongols, in History of the Mongols* by Bertold Spuler, trans. Helga and Stuart Drummond, London: Routledge and Kegan Paul, 1972, p. 74.

belief was that specialized holy men called shamans could make contact with the spirits. Through dreams and waking visions, a shaman, or *kam*, could make known the spirits' feelings and opinions.

Showing respect for the ancestral spirits of one's family on a daily basis was particularly important. Aiding in this aspect of Mongol spiritualism were effigies, figurines or other images representing those spirits. Lane explains,

> The family often kept expensively dressed effigies of their ancestors in specially assigned places in their [houses]. When they traveled, the effigies, which the Mongols called *ongghot*, were placed in a special wagon under the supervision of the shamans. ... These *ongghot* were made of felt. Both the master and mistress of the tent had an *ongghot* hung on the wall of the [house] above their designated position,

and other smaller effigies would be placed nearer the entrance.[16]

Still another aspect of traditional Mongol shamanism was the belief that shamans could foretell certain future events. This included determining lucky and unlucky days and planning ahead so that important undertakings would happen only on the lucky days. Mongol leaders rarely fought battles on days deemed unlucky by the shamans. Thus, shamans wielded considerable influence and power within Mongol society. Sometimes, in fact, a holy man held too much influence for his own good. For example, when Genghis Khan concluded that his leading shaman had become too powerful, Khan had him killed. This was only one of numerous audacious, cold-blooded acts committed by the greatest leader the Mongols ever produced, a man whose story continues to be told and retold nearly eight centuries after his death.

Chapter Two

The Rise of Genghis Khan

odern estimates for the birth year of medieval Asia's greatest conqueror and ruler range from as early as 1155 to as late as 1167. The date most often cited by scholars is 1162, but the exact year will likely never be known for sure. More certain is the approximate location of his birth—the banks of the Onon River, in northern Mongolia, not far from a mountain called Burkhan Khaldun. Several members of the Borjigin clan, one of many small bands of nomadic Mongols then roaming the steppes, were camped beside the river. Among them were the clan leader, Yesugei (or Yesukhei), and his pregnant wife, Hoelun. After Hoelun gave birth, she and Yesugei named the baby boy Temujin (or Temuchin), which in their language means "iron worker." Noted French historian René Grousset remarked how fitting it was that "the future 'Conqueror of the World' should be marked out [by] name as a man of iron, whose [later] work it was to forge a new Asia."[17]

Indeed, the boy Temujin was destined to later acquire the title Genghis Khan (pronounced CHING-gis KAHN) and to conquer almost all of Asia. As a child, however, he at first gave little hint of the extraordinary leadership skills he would display as an adult. In fact, his beginnings were humble and unremarkable, even obscure and poverty-stricken by modern American standards.

Still, looking back on Temujin's life from a modern vantage, one can understand how his childhood laid much of the groundwork for his manhood. It is easy to see, for instance, how the harsh, even cruel conditions of his youth shaped him into a tough, hard-edged man with tremendously strong survival abilities and savvy insights into life and people. As scholar Jack Weatherford points out,

A Vision Reveals Temujin's Fate

According to *The Secret History of the Mongols*, a respected Mongol named Khorchi, of the Bagarin tribe, had a dream vision in which he realizes that the young Temujin was destined to rule all the Mongols. Khorchi said,

> A sign from Heaven came to me in a dream and told me that Temujin was meant to be our leader. In this dream I saw a great cow enter our camp. First she circled Jamuka, then she charged at his tent … kicking up dust clouds with her hooves, with one crooked horn on her head. Then an ox with no horns at all pulled up to the tent stake and harnessed himself to the cart until he came up to Temujin. He stopped there and began bellowing, "Heaven and Earth have agreed that Temujin should be Lord of the Nation. I've come to bring you the nation." These are the signs I've seen and the dreams I've received.

Quoted in Paul Kahn, ed., *The Secret History of the Mongols: The Origin of Chingis Khan*, Boston: Cheng and Tsui, 1998, p. 43.

The boy who became Genghis Khan grew up in a world of excessive tribal violence, including murder, kidnapping, and enslavement. [From] this harsh setting, he learned, in dreadful detail, the full range of human emotion: desire, ambition, and cruelty. … Under such horrific conditions, the boy showed an instinct for survival and self-preservation [and] the dual capacity for friendship and enmity [hatred] forged in [his] youth endured throughout his life and became the defining trait of his character.[18]

One must be careful, however, not to delve too far into a person's childhood for incidents predicting his or her future. Ancient and medieval writers were always anxious to discover omens, or signs with which to predict the future. And when they could not find any, they sometimes quietly inserted them after the fact. This seems to have happened in Temujin's case, for the thirteenth-century text *The Secret History of the Mongols* alleges that his birth was far from ordinary. It reads, "As he was born, he emerged clutching a blood clot the size of a knucklebone [an animal bone] in his right hand."[19] Modern scholars suspect that this detail was fabricated later in order to give the impression that even as a fetus Temujin was fierce and warlike.

Abandonment and Murder

Almost nothing certain is known about Temujin's earliest years. The first substantial and well-documented incident in his life occurred when he was nine years old, at which time his father decided to begin arranging the boy's future marriage. Yesugei took Temujin to the camp of the Onggirat, a hill tribe. Its leader, Dai Sechen, had a ten-year-old daughter named Borte. Yesugei and Dai came to an agreement in which Temujin would live with the Onggirat for a few years while learning the skills of warrior and diplomat. Eventually he would marry Borte and return to his own clan.

It remains unknown how Temujin felt about this arrangement. But whatever he thought soon became irrelevant because news came that on his way home Yesugei had been poisoned by some Tatars he had met on the steppes. Temujin rushed back to his family to find that his father had just died. Making matters worse, the men who had earlier followed Yesugei had decided to desert and join a rival clan, the Tayichiguds. Perhaps because they knew the Tayichiguds would not take in the family of a former adversary, the deserters now abandoned Temujin's family. In addition to Temujin and his mother, the family consisted of another of Yesugei's wives and the boy's three brothers, two half brothers, and sister. For the next few years, Hoelun and the other woman scrounged for berries, roots, fish, mice, and whatever else they could find to feed the family, which, thanks to them, survived.

Yesugei Meets Borte

The Secret History of the Mongols contains this account of how Temujin's father, Yesugei, met Borte, the young woman who would eventually become Temujin's wife.

[Borte's father, Dei, said] "My friend Yesugei, let's go to my tent. I've got a young daughter there. My friend should meet her." Dei the Wise led Yesugei's horse to his tent and helped him dismount. When Yesugei saw Dei's daughter, he was impressed. She was a girl whose face filled with light, whose eyes filled with fire, and he began to consider her father's proposal [that she marry Temujin]. She was ten years old, a year older than Temujin, and her name was Borte. After spending the night in the tent, the next morning Yesugei asked Dei for his daughter['s hand in a marriage with his son Temujin].

Paul Kahn, ed., *The Secret History of the Mongols: The Origin of Chingis Khan*, Boston: Cheng and Tsui, 1998, pp. 14–15.

Genghis Khan is estimated to have been born in 1162 in northern Mongolia.

In the meantime, Temujin became blood brother, or *anda*, with Jamuka (or Jamugha), a slightly older boy. Jamuka belonged to the same tribe but a different clan whose members were distantly related to Temujin's family. In the ceremony of blood brotherhood, each boy swallowed some of the other's blood. It was thought that in this way they exchanged a small part of each other's soul. The *Secret History* tells how Temujin and Jamuka first became *andas* when they were eleven years old and how not long afterward they renewed this special bond. It reads,

When the two were off in the forest together shooting arrows, Jamuka took two pieces of calf horn. He bored holes in them, glued them together to fashion a whistling arrowhead, and gave this arrow as a present to Temujin. In return, Temujin gave him a beautiful arrow with a Cyprus wood tip. With that exchange of arrows, they declared themselves *andas* a second time. So Temujin and Jamuka said to each other: "We've heard the elders say, 'when two men become *anda* their lives become one. One will never desert the other and will always defend him.' This is the way we'll act from now on. We'll renew our old pledge and love each other forever."[20]

At that moment, Temujin had no way of knowing that when the two were older, Jamuka would turn on him, breaking their solemn pledge and sending Temujin's life in a new direction.

Even while the young Temujin was enjoying his feelings of brotherhood with Jamuka, he came to bitterly resent one of his real half brothers, Bekhter. Because he was the oldest male in the family, Bekhter felt he had a right to order his relatives around. He also began taking more than his fair share of what little food they had, so most of them came to dislike him intensely. One day Bekhter stole some food from Temujin, who was then about fifteen. And Temujin and his full brother Kasar retaliated. Using their bows and arrows, they killed their half brother. Although Hoelun, too, had resented Bekhter, she was outraged that her sons had slain a family member and told them in a loud voice,

Killers, both of you! When he came out screaming from the heat of my womb, this one [Temujin] was holding a clot of black blood in his hand. And now you've both destroyed without thinking, like the [dog] who eats its own afterbirth, like the panther that needlessly leaps from a cliff, like the lion that can't control its own fury ... like the wolf who hides himself in the blizzard to hunt down his prey ... you've killed your own brother![21]

Captivity and Escape

When the leader of the Tayichigud clan, Targutai, heard what Temujin had done, he saw an opportunity to cripple a potential rival. Targutai knew that, with Bekhter out of the way, Temujin was now the male head of Yesugei's family. As a former rival of Yesugei, Targutai worried that over time Temujin might become as popular a leader as his father had been, which might pose a threat to Targutai's authority in his own clan. For these reasons, Targutai wanted to get rid of Temujin. But he knew he could not simply kill the young man, for that carried the risk that Targutai would then be assassinated by one of Temujin's revenge-seeking relatives.

Targutai's solution was to render Temujin helpless by capturing him and turning him into a slave. Claiming that the younger man had committed murder on lands the Tayichigud often used for camping and hunting, Targutai ordered his warriors to find and seize Temujin.

The latter tried to escape, but he encountered several setbacks, including a broken saddle. The old Mongol proverb about things going badly if one's horse was not in top form now proved painfully true. The young man was forced to hide in the woods for three nights. And when he again attempted to flee, his pursuers closed in. According to the *Secret History*,

> As he neared the edge of the forest, a white boulder the size of a tent fell down in the path and blocked the way out. He said to himself: "I think Heaven wants me to stay here," and for three more nights he stayed in the woods. For nine nights now he'd been without food and he said to himself: "I don't want to die here, forgotten and nameless. I've got to escape." He cut a new path around the boulder using the knife he carried to cut himself arrows. The brush was so thick there, he couldn't push through until he'd hacked a new path. But as he led his horse out, the Tayichigud were still waiting. They captured him there and took him away.[22]

When the captors took Temujin to their camp, they picked up a large wooden yoke normally used to hitch oxen and tied it to his shoulders and arms. That way he could neither use his hands nor stand up straight. Every day members of the clan laughed and hurled insults at the young man, who was in constant pain as a result of the heavy yoke he bore on his shoulders. Fortunately for Temujin, however, one of the warriors, a man named Sorkhan, who had known and liked the captive's father, took pity on him. Each night, Sorkhan and his sons brought Temujin into their tent and removed the yoke. This allowed the young man to get some decent sleep.

Eventually, Temujin planned an escape. He chose a time when a guard was leading him around on a rope attached to the yoke. Gathering his nerve and strength, the captive made his move. Scholar Peter Brent writes,

Temujin pulled away, jerked the cord from the other's hand, then flung himself forward and sideways as the other bent to retrieve it, his wooden collar transformed into a club. The blow smashed into the [guard's] uncovered skull ... and the dark night swung open like a door. Temujin ran, the river bank his guide. Before word spread in the camp that he had escaped, he had hidden himself in the stream, forcing himself into the darkness and moon-reflections of the water.[23]

After searchers had passed by the stream, Temujin shrewdly returned to the camp, knowing that it was the last place they would expect him to be. There, Sorkhan kindly removed the yoke and hid him in a cart near the family's lodge. Later, Sorkhan and his sons gave Temujin some food and weapons and sent him on his way.

A Newfound Reputation

Free of the Tayichiguds, Temujin, now sixteen, decided to find his intended bride, Borte, and, if possible, marry her. In time he was able to locate her tribe, the Onggirat, and was pleased to find that Borte, who liked him, had long been hoping he would return for her. Not only that, she and her kinsmen were greatly impressed by the young man's recent adventures, particularly his daring escape from the Tayichiguds.

Indeed, to his surprise Temujin found that he had become a sort of local folk hero. Part of his newfound reputation was based on the fact that, though he was still young, in Mongol eyes he cut an imposing and in some ways exciting figure. Already he displayed many of the qualities he would later demonstrate as a major political and military leader. A contemporary description of Temujin's physical appearance and character has survived. It was penned by a thirteenth-century Persian chronicler, Minhaj al-Siraj Juzjani, who writes, "[Temujin was] a man of tall stature, of vigorous build, robust in body, the hair on his face scanty ... with cat's eyes, possessed of great energy, discernment [judgment], genius and understanding, awe-inspiring ... just, resolute, an overthrower of enemies, [and] intrepid."[24]

Happy to welcome such an impressive individual into their family, Borte's relatives wasted no time in seeing that she and Temujin were married. Part of her dowry (valuables given by her father for maintenance in the marriage) consisted of a beautiful coat made of

Even in his teen years, Genghis Khan displayed many of the qualities that would make him a major political and military leader.

sable fur. The couple decided to use the coat as a gift to seal an alliance with a man named Toghrul, today more often remembered as Ong Khan. The widely respected leader of the powerful Kerait (or Kereit) tribe, Ong Khan was an old friend and former *anda* of Temujin's father, Yesugei. Accepting Temujin as a kind of foster son, Ong Khan promised to aid him in reuniting the scattered members of the fractured Borjigin clan.

As it turned out, Ong Khan immediately became more useful to Temujin in a way that neither man had expected. Another powerful tribe, the Merkid (or Merkit), had maintained a longstanding grudge against the Borjigin clan. The reason was that many years before, Temujin's father had stolen a Merkid woman, none other than Hoelun, who had become Temujin's mother. Hoping to finally attain vengeance, not long after Temujin and Borte were married the Merkid kidnapped Borte.

The enraged Temujin quickly began recruiting fighters to rescue his wife. He also sought the aid of Ong Khan, who rallied many of his own warriors. In addition, having heard what was happening, Temujin's *anda*, Jamuka, arrived with more horsemen to swell the ranks of the growing army. As these forces approached the enemy camp, many Merkid soldiers fled. And those who remained were easily defeated, which led to Borte's rescue. The *Secret History* captures the thrilling moment when the lovers were reunited:

Temujin rode through the retreating [Merkid] camp, shouting out:

"Borte! Borte!" Borte was among the Merkid who ran in the darkness, and when she … recognized Temujin's voice, Borte leaped from the cart. … All about them was moonlight. As Temujin looked down … he recognized Borte [and] in a moment he was down from his horse and they were in each other's arms, embracing. … "I've found what I came for," [he said]. This is how Temujin found Borte, saving her from the Merkid.[25]

Wars with Former Friends

The victory over the Merkid further increased Temujin's reputation as a skilled, daring leader. Hoping to exploit this popularity, he began to maneuver himself to become the ruler of all the Mongol tribes. First, he sent out riders, who asked people in various clans and tribes to join his group, which was essentially a new tribe. Many warriors accepted and brought their families to his camp. Temujin also used more blatant means of finding recruits. For instance he gave horses or fine furs to some prospective followers and promised leadership positions to others.

In addition, year after year Temujin enacted social and military reforms that impressed his followers and cemented their loyalty. He reorganized his tribe, assigning everyone specific tasks, which made both the camp and the army more efficient and productive. He also formed a personal bodyguard squad made up of young Mongol men

وبوصنی کنام آن بیدی نورتافت باجاموذ مصاف داد واوراشکت و نؤم قنفرات همانجا بابلی اوان

Although Genghis Khan was a shrewd fighter, he showed mercy by enacting a policy in which defeated opponents were welcomed into his growing tribe.

who became skilled fighters and were steadfastly loyal to him. In addition, Temujin promised his followers that they would share in the spoils gained during any and all future military campaigns. Perhaps most crucially, he enacted a policy in which defeated opponents were not driven away, as was the traditional custom, but rather welcomed into the growing tribe. These and other reforms showed Temujin to be a resourceful, forward-thinking, and inspiring leader. And he steadily drew more and more steppe clans to his banners. Brent writes, "There were now, indeed, a [great many] heroes and chieftains in the new clan, proud rivals all,

men of ambition based on blood, power, and established wealth. None would serve under any of the others. [But] all might serve under Temujin ... supported by his recent success."[26] The members of his group saw him as such a natural leader, in fact, that they started calling him khan, or overall boss.

While Temujin was reorganizing and expanding his new tribe, he found to his dismay that his relationship with his old friend Jamuka was changing for the worse. After Borte's rescue from the Merkid, the two men renewed their blood brotherhood. But in the two years that followed, they steadily became rivals and eventually they declared war on

Temujin Receives the Title of Khan

After leading a large group of Mongols for a few years, Temujin was named overall leader, or khan. According to a passage in *The Secret History of the Mongols*, the clan leaders told him:

We want you to be Khan. Temujin, if you'll be our Khan, we'll search [for] the beautiful women and virgins, for the great palace tents, [for] the finest geldings and mares. We'll gather all these and bring them to you. When we go off to hunt for wild game, we'll go out first to drive them together for you to kill. ... If we disobey your command during battle, take away our possessions, our children, and wives. Leave us behind in the dust, cutting off our heads where we stand and letting them fall to the ground. If we disobey your council in peacetime, take away our tents and our goods, our wives, and our children. Leave us behind when you move, abandoned in the desert without a protector.

Quoted in Paul Kahn, ed., *The Secret History of the Mongols: The Origin of Chingis Khan*, Boston: Cheng and Tsui, 1998, pp. 44–45.

each other. Jamuka, who controlled more clans than Temujin, won the first battle. Intent on sending his former *anda* the message that he was a force to be reckoned with, Jamuka boiled seventy of Temujin's followers to death in large cooking cauldrons.

In 1201 the combined forces of Temujin and Ong Khan soundly defeated Jamuka, and Temujin absorbed most of Jamuka's surviving fighters into his own army. Jamuka escaped and began to regroup his forces.

In the meantime, Ong Khan's son, Senggum, began worrying that his father might push him aside in favor of his foster son, Temujin. Senggum therefore convinced his father to turn on Temujin. In 1203 Ong Khan and Senggum attacked Temujin, but the latter managed to counterattack and defeat them. Ong Khan was killed, his son fled into the wilderness, and Temujin disbanded their tribe, the Kerait.

The following year, Temujin once more met Jamuka in battle and Jamuka again was defeated. This time, however, he was captured. In what most of those present saw as an amazing display of forgiveness and generosity, Temujin said that if Jamuka swore allegiance to him once more and never again broke his oath, he would be allowed to live. But, according to the *Secret History*, the disgraced Jamuka declined, saying,

What good would I be as your ally? I'd only invade your dreams in the dark night and trouble your thoughts in the day. [I] went wrong when I strove to be a better man than my *anda*. [You] whose destiny is Heaven's will, have surpassed me in everything. My *anda*, if you want to favor me, then let me die quickly. [Please] see that it is done without shedding my blood. Once I am dead and my bones have been buried high on a cliff, I will protect your seed. I will become a prayer to protect you.[27]

Following his former friend's wishes, Temujin had Jamuka wrapped in a blanket and crushed to death. This form of execution, in which none of the condemned man's blood spilled onto the ground, was considered becoming of a warrior.

Unity at Last

The defeat and death of Jamuka eliminated one of the last credible obstacles to Temujin's goal of becoming leader of all the Mongol clans. Two years later, in 1206, representatives from every Mongol group assembled in a large meeting called a *kuriltai*. By this time all agreed that unity would serve them well and that Temujin had by far the best chance to maintain such unity. According to one modern expert,

The tribes believed that unity under Genghis would bring them power and wealth. As long as Genghis delivered, the tribes would remain loyal, and it was Genghis Khan's dilemma to ensure that he could continue to deliver booty, power, and prestige, without which his empire would unravel and his position would be challenged.[28]

Already the khan of his own group of followers, Temujin now became khan of all the Mongols. The leaders of the clans swore an oath of loyalty to him and loudly proclaimed him Genghis Khan, meaning "Oceanic Ruler" or "Universal Leader." Many of those in attendance likely assumed they were witnessing their leader's moment of greatest triumph. But they were wrong. In truth, his incredible list of accomplishments had only just begun to be written.

Chapter Three

Military and Legal Reforms

When Temujin accepted the title of Genghis Khan in 1206, he initiated his reign as the first ever ruler of the united Mongol clans and tribes. Unlike the rulers of China, India, Persia, and the European states, however, he had no country to lead, for although there was a Mongol people, there had never been a formal Mongol nation. To remedy this situation, that same year he announced the formation of the *Yeke Mongol Ulus*, or Great Mongol Nation. It was understood that the territories making up that nation, or empire, would be any and all of those the Mongols claimed and occupied. At the moment, they occupied a large portion of the Mongolian steppes. But later, Genghis Khan hoped, many other lands would be added to his empire.

The Great Khan, as many came to call him, realized that another crucial aspect of building his new nation was to ensure the continued unity of his people.

Solemn ceremonies and oaths of loyalty like those that took place in 1206 were all well and good. But he knew it would take much more to maintain the Mongols' existing unity. Specifically, it would entail stronger, more efficient organization of his new army and new laws to regulate the people and give them a sense of shared values and purpose. "For his nation-state to survive," scholar Jack Weatherford writes,

> he needed to build strong institutions, and for Genghis Khan this began with the army that brought him to power. He made it even stronger and more central to government. [Also] to maintain peace in this large and ethnically diverse set of tribes that he had forged into a nation, he quickly proclaimed new laws to suppress the traditional causes of tribal feuding and war.[29]

Improved Organization

Throughout history many kings, military generals, and other leaders have tried to make their armies stronger and more efficient. Some have succeeded in these endeavors and others have failed. Fortunately for Genghis Khan, he possessed an advantage over the vast majority of these leaders, namely a brilliant natural grasp of military affairs, which he had repeatedly demonstrated while unifying the Mongols. Indeed, scholar J.J Saunders points out, "The authority of Genghis [Khan] was now securely based on his personal prowess in war."[30]

Among the first and most important military reforms the Mongol ruler instituted was a more systematic and efficient organization of the troops, who were nearly all cavalry, or mounted soldiers. No one knows how many troops Genghis Khan fielded at this time (or any time) because figures for the Mongol population in that era are unknown. The most common estimated figures for Mongol armies are twenty to thirty thousand men (although some historians claim somewhat larger figures). Khan divided these fighters into units delineated by the decimal system, that is, multiples of ten. The largest unit was the *tumen* (or *touman*), consisting of ten thousand men. According to historian James Chambers,

> Each *tumen* was divided into ten regiments of a thousand men called

Genghis Khan divided the Mongol troops into specific units, which made the Mongol army organized and efficient.

Mongol Defensive Gear

Norwegian researcher Per Inge Oestmoen, an expert on the Mongols, here describes some of the main items of defensive gear used by Mongol soldiers:

The Mongol warrior used to wear Chinese silk underwear, if it could be obtained. One would not normally consider underwear to be military equipment, but the fact is that silk is a very tough substance. If arrows are shot from a larger distance, they will not easily penetrate the silk. Even if an arrow penetrates the human skin, the silk may hold, so that the arrow can be drawn out from the wound by pulling the silk around. This would also prevent poison from entering the bloodstream. Outside the normal clothes, the warrior carried a protective shield of light yet effective leather armor, which was impregnated with a lacquer-like substance in order to make it more impervious to penetration by arrows, swords and knives, and also to protect it against humid weather. ... Often their horses also carried this type of leather armor. The horses also had saddles with stirrups, because this was necessary in order to carry all the equipment and to fight from the saddle. Mongol warriors also wore helmets, the upper part of which was made of metal. The parts covering the ears and neck were [made of] leather.

Per Inge Oestmoen, "The Mongol Military Might," The Realm of the Mongols, www.coldsiberia.org/monmight.htm.

minghans, each *minghan* contained ten squadrons of a hundred men called *jaguns* and each *jagun* was divided into ten troops of ten men called *arbans*. The ten men in each *arban* elected their own commander and the ten commanders of the *arbans* elected the commander of the *jagun*. Beyond that the commanders of the *minghans* and *tumens* were appointed by the khan himself and given the military rank of *noyan*.[31]

The *noyans* and other military officers were the key to keeping the various army units well ordered and efficient. First, these commanders immediately and strictly followed their superiors' orders, which ensured that every man in the army would carry out the khan's strategy promptly and accurately. Another reform called for promoting these officers according to their abilities and merit, instead of their family connections or other political factors. This made it much more likely that talented, hard-working, effective commanders would be in charge of the army on all levels. Moreover, their duties extended beyond the battlefield itself, where they fought right alongside their men. For example, the officers often inspected weapons and supplies before and after a battle and sternly punished any men who avoided their responsibilities.

Discipline and Training

Other military reforms dealt with training the soldiers and preparing them as well as possible for the rigors of battle. Fortunately for Genghis Khan and his officers, they had a considerable head start in this effort. Toughness, discipline, and courage were drilled into most Mongol men from an early age, so a good deal of their military training came from their upbringing and life lessons.

The famous Venetian merchant and traveler Marco Polo, who saw the Mongol army firsthand several years after Genghis Khan's reign, commented on the amazing toughness and discipline displayed by each Mongol fighter:

> They are [more] capable of hardships than [the soldiers of] other nations; for many a time, if need be, they will go for a month without any supply of food, living only on the milk of their mares and on such game as their bows may win them. [And] in case of great urgency they will ride ten days on end without lighting a fire or taking a meal. ... In truth, they are stout and valiant soldiers, and inured to [hardened by] war.[32]

Polo was also impressed at how brave and loyal Khan's troops were. He observed that they seemed to rush into battle with no thought for their own safety and were willing to risk life and limb for their emperor. "Never were men seen," Polo writes, "who did such feats of arms for the love and honour of their Lord, as these had done [in] battle."[33]

A more formal kind of training for the soldiers consisted of what the Mongols called the Great Hunt. A huge, long-term hunting expedition held once each year, it gave the men a feeling for the physical and emotional challenges they would face later in battle. Chambers explains,

> The great hunt [was] designed to generate a "team spirit" throughout the army, temper its discipline, and swell its morale. For the Mongols, no other sport or military exercise could have been more effective. It was held at the beginning of each winter in peacetime, lasted for three months, and involved every soldier. Huntsmen marked out a starting line, up to eighty miles long, with flags denoting the assembly points for each *tumen*, and hundreds of miles ahead of the line they planted another flag to mark the finishing point. ... The entire army, fully armed and dressed for battle, would ride forward in one line, driving all the game before it. As the weeks went by and the game began to build up, the wings of the army would advance ahead of the center, and when they had passed the

finishing point, would begin to ride in to meet each other, totally encircling the game. Once the wings had met, the circle would begin to contract with the line deepening, until, on the last day of the drive, the Mongol army became a huge human amphitheatre with thousands of terrified animals crowded into its arena.[34]

The Lethal Mongol Bow

Genghis Khan also made sure that his troops were well armed, both during their training for war and on the battlefield itself. Each fighter had a bronze or iron sword and sometimes a battle-ax and a lance as well. The lance was a long spear that a cavalryman used to spike opposing horsemen or infantrymen (foot soldiers).

Although these arms were important to Mongol warriors, their most reliable and effective weapon was the composite bow. It consisted of several different materials combined to produce the maximum achievable amount of power and accuracy. Many of the Mongols' adversaries used ordinary bows—called either self-bows or simple bows. Such weapons utilized a single piece of wood. Mongol composite bows, by contrast, were constructed from two or more types of wood, along with animal horn

Mongol troops were well armed for battle. Each soldier carried a bronze or iron sword, sometimes a battle-ax, and a lance like the one pictured.

The composite bows used by Mongol warriors were the strongest, most advanced bows in the world at that time.

and sinew (tendons). The horn gave the bow extra strength, while the sinew produced added springing power. A soldier or other weapons maker pieced these materials together with extremely strong glue derived from boiled fish bladders.

Modern weapons experts say that the bows created in this manner were the finest bows in the world before the advent of more technologically advanced versions in the twentieth century. Consider the case of the renowned English longbow, used in the same period as the Mongol composite bow. The longbow could shoot an arrow up to 750 feet (229m). Although this is certainly impressive, it did

not match the power of the Mongol bow, which fired arrows up to 1,050 feet (320m). Mongol archers often achieved astounding accuracy, killing or wounding enemy fighters from great distances.

Also, the manner in which the Great Khan's soldiers used their bows in battle was no less remarkable. A typical Mongol horseman was able to turn in the saddle and fire backwards at an opponent. The same rider could coordinate the release of his arrow with his horse's movements. One impressive trick was to release the arrow during the split second when all four of the animal's hooves were off the ground. This greatly diminished the

Mongol Offensive Weapons

Timothy May, who teaches history at North Georgia College and State University, offers this overview of the principal offensive weapons wielded by the Mongols:

Each Mongol warrior had more than one bow and used a variety of arrows with specialized purposes.

> The armament of the Mongols focused on the bow. This was a double recurve composite bow, made of layers of sinew, horn, and wood. Each warrior had more than one, probably attached, in a special quiver, to their saddles on each horse in addition to quivers of arrows. The bow itself possessed an incredible amount of penetrating power, often consisting of pull-weights of over one hundred pounds. The Mongols used a wide variety of arrows, many with specialized purposes, such as armor piercing, blunt stun arrows, and even whistling arrows for signaling purposes. In addition, the soldiers carried sabers, maces, axes, and sometimes a short spear with a hook at the bottom of the blade. Other supplies, such as rope, rations, files for sharpening arrows, etc., were also carried. This made the soldiers of the Mongol army a self-sufficient unit able to function independently of supply lines. Thus, they were not hampered by a slow moving baggage train, allowing them to make the rapid marches that so characterized Mongol warfare.

Timothy May, "Mongol Arms," San Antonio College, www.alamo.edu/sac/history/keller/mongols/empsub2.html.

vibrations that would otherwise have reduced the accuracy of the shot.

Frequently the Mongol riders fired their arrows from a considerable distance. Often a large shower of well-aimed arrows proved enough to frighten enemy soldiers and encourage them to flee the battlefield. If this approach did not work, the khan or another Mongol commander might order his men to move in and employ their other weapons. In his book, *The Travels of Marco Polo* Marco Polo describes a battle in which both firing arrows from a distance and close-in fighting occurred:

A fierce and bloody conflict began. The air was instantly filled with a cloud of arrows that poured down on every side [and] the loud cries and shouts of the men, together with the noise of the horses and weapons, were such as to inspire terror. … When their arrows had been discharged [from a distance, they then moved closer and] engaged in close combat with their lances [and] swords. … Such was the slaughter, and so large were the heaps of [bodies] that it became impossible for the one [side] to advance upon the other.[35]

Battlefield Tactics

In addition to their efficient organization and highly effective weapons, Genghis Khan's warriors learned to perform a number of battlefield tactics and

Mongol fighters were such expert horsemen that they could move with amazing speed, allowing them to take their enemies by surprise.

maneuvers that frequently dazzled and frightened their opponents. First, Mongol fighters were such expert horsemen and their mounts were so strong and well trained that they could move with what was then seen as amazing speed. As Marco Polo tells it, this often allowed them to take advantage of the element of surprise:

> The Great Kaan's [Khan's] forces arrived so fast and so suddenly that the others knew nothing of the matter. For the Kaan had caused such strict watch to be made in every direction [that] every [enemy scout] that appeared was instantly captured. Thus [the enemy] had no warning of [the Mongol army's] coming and was completely taken by surprise. ... So thus you see why it was that the [Great Khan] equipped his force with such speed and secrecy.[36]

Other common Mongol tactics were part of what modern military experts call stealth warfare. Whenever possible Mongol soldiers avoided fighting the enemy in hand-to-hand combat and employed some form of deception instead. Perhaps their favorite tactic was the feigned, or fake, retreat. Military historian John R. Elting writes,

> Chinese [and other opposing] armies of infantry and chariots seldom caught up with them [the Mongols]. When they did, the [Mongols'] normal strategy was to retreat slowly, luring the [enemy] out into the wastelands where fatigue, hunger, and thirst would make them easy prey. ... A favorite ruse was a feigned retreat to draw the enemy into broken or barren country, where his forces would soon become disorganized and exhausted.[37]

Another modern expert explains the psychological aspect of the tactic:

> This maneuver was often interpreted as implying cowardice and lack of strength. In reality, the Mongols wanted the [opposing] forces to pursue them, and thus expose their weaknesses. This is the Asiatic principle, known from martial arts like ju jitsu and kung fu, of being soft and yielding where the opponent is strong, and be hard and offensive at spots where weakness is encountered. This principle was developed into a fine art by the Mongols. The principle of brute strength, heavy swords, and armor is effective in narrow streets of cities [and] inside castles and fortresses, but in the open field it pays off to be nimble, smart and alert.[38]

There were other variants of the feigned retreat. In one, a retreating Mongol force lured its pursuers into an ambush in which a second Mongol regiment appeared, seemingly out of nowhere. Still another version of the tactic was for the Mongols to retreat so quickly that the pursuers would lose their trail. Thinking the Mongols were long gone, the enemy soldiers would stop and make camp, letting down their guard in the process. Then, a day or two later the Mongols would sneak back and surround and attack their unsuspecting opponents.

In these and other ways, the Mongols became a military power to be reckoned with. Their superior organization and tactics struck fear into their enemies and elevated the reputation of their greatest commander, Genghis Khan, to legendary status. In the words of renowned American general Douglas MacArthur:

> Were the accounts of all battles, save only those of Genghis Khan, effaced [erased] from the pages of history ... the [modern student of military history] would still possess a mine of untold wealth. ... The successes of that amazing leader, beside which the triumphs of most other commanders in history pale into insignificance, are proof sufficient of his unerring instinct for the fundamental qualifications of an army [and] these conceptions [remain] as kernels of eternal truth, as applicable today [as] they were when, seven centuries ago, the great Mongol applied them to the discomfiture and amazement of a terrified world.[39]

Laws and Justice

Paralleling and in some ways complementing Genghis Khan's military reforms were his legal ones. More than any other single factor, his system of laws (*yasa*) and justice demonstrated to surprised foreign visitors that the Mongols were not unruly savages, but instead civilized individuals who respected the rule of law. The Great Khan's laws were not only written down, or codified, they were also consistently applied to all members of society, regardless of social status and wealth, and nearly always enforced.

The sweeping law code that Genghis Khan introduced a little at a time between 1206 and 1218 became known as the Great Yasa. He knew that to issue official laws, he needed an official written language. So he ordered a scribe to create a writing system for the spoken Mongolian tongue. The language was based on the script of Uyghur, a Turkic language spoken in parts of Mongolia and China that featured an alphabet derived from Arabic. The new Mongolian writing system, which many centuries later became known as Classic Mongolian Script, came to be used for all of the Great Khan's official documents.

No all-inclusive copy of the final document has survived the ravages of time. But some hefty portions of it did endure in the works of foreigners who visited the Mongol realm. One was Marco Polo, who visited the palace of Genghis Khan's grandson, Kublai Khan. The Mongol empire was then divided into thirty-four provinces, each administered by twelve governors. In addition, each province had a legal official who, aided by several clerks, ran a local court that administered justice to the people.

Not surprisingly, some of the laws upheld by these courts were based on ancient tribal customs. And because they were so old and connected to specific local traditions, they appeared rather strange to outside observers. One of these visitors was the Persian historian Ata-Malik Juvaini, whose book, *The History of the World-Conqueror*, remains one of the key medieval sources about the Mongol Empire. Juvaini writes,

> It is laid down in the *yasa* [of] the Mongols that in the seasons of spring and summer no one may sit in water by day, nor wash his hands in a stream, nor draw water in gold or silver vessels, nor lay out washed garments on the plain, it being their belief that such actions increased the thunder and lightning.[40]

Although these rules may sound silly, many other Mongol laws were more sensible and practical. Some also closely mirrored some of the precepts in the sacred books of the Jews, Christians, and Muslims. For instance, one Mongol law forbade lying. Another made it illegal to commit adultery. Still another ordained that a person must treat a neighbor as he or she would want to be treated by that neighbor. In addition, there were humane statutes calling for people to respect and give aid to elderly and impoverished members of society.

Several other laws Genghis Khan enacted were influenced by his own experiences as a young man. According to scholar Frank E. Smitha:

The kidnapping of women had caused feuding among the Mongols, and, as a teenager, Temujin had suffered from the kidnapping of his young wife, Borte. [Partly for that reason] he made it law that there was to be no kidnapping of women. [Furthermore] he declared all children legitimate, whomever the mother. He made it law that no woman would be sold into marriage. The stealing of animals had caused dissension among the Mongols, and Genghis Khan made it a capital offense. A lost animal was to be returned to its owner, and taking lost property as one's own was to be considered thievery and a capital offense. Genghis Khan [also] regulated hunting—a winter activity—improving the availability of meat for everyone.[41]

Mongols were not the only ones expected to follow Genghis Khan's laws. Visiting foreigners were also subject to them, as illustrated by an incident that William of Rubruck, a European monk, witnessed. He and his fellow Europeans were at the royal court of Mongke Khan, one of Genghis Khan's grandsons, where a translator told the visitors that touching the borders of the entrance to the khan's home was against the law (except, of course, for the ruler himself). William and his companions managed not to touch the threshold on their way in; but as they exited, one of them accidentally brushed up against it. For a while, it appeared that the guilty party might be punished. But William himself went to the local judge and claimed that the translator had not explained the law well enough. It was a testament to the flexibility and fairness of Mongol justice that the judge ordered that William's friend be released.

Penalties for Lawbreakers

William's friend was fortunate that he was acquitted. If he had been convicted, he would have been executed. Indeed, the death penalty was prescribed for breaking several of the laws of the Great Yasa. Among the other capital offenses (those punishable by death) were murder, adultery, employing sorcery to harm someone, and declaring bankruptcy three times. As for the methods of execution, average citizens were usually beheaded or hacked to death with swords. Individuals of high military or social rank, on the other hand, could request a so-called bloodless death, such as being wrapped in a carpet and crushed, as Genghis Khan's former friend Jamuka had been.

A good many other crimes were punished by less drastic means. One common penalty for minor crimes was paying a fine. The payment could be in the form of objects of value, as in the case of a horse thief, who was required to return the stolen horse along with nine

A Mongol Leader Shows Mercy

Mongol justice was frequently severe. Nevertheless, sometimes Mongol leaders, including Genghis Khan, showed mercy if they felt the situation called for it. Such a situation is cited in the writings of medieval Persian historian Ata-Malik Juvaini, who describes Mongol society at length. Juvaini claims that Genghis Khan's son, Ogedei, who succeeded his father as khan, ordered the execution of three men who had committed a serious crime. Then Ogedei noticed a woman who was crying and asked what was bothering her. She told him,

"Of those men whom you ordered to be put to death, one is my husband, another is my son, and the third my brother." "Choose one of them," said Ogedei, "and for your sake he shall be spared." "I can find a substitute for my husband," replied the woman, "and children, too, I can hope for. But for a brother there can be no substitute." [Hearing this, Ogedei] spared the lives of all three.

Quoted in Bertold Spuler, *History of the Mongols*, trans. Helga and Stuart Drummond, London: Routledge and Kegan Paul, 1989, p. 63.

others of equal value. Another frequent punishment for lesser offenses was receiving a beating with wooden rods.

The Great Khan's penalties might seem overly harsh in modern eyes. But they were fitting for their time and place—the medieval Asian steppes, where life was tough and demanding and no police or prisons existed to maintain order. More importantly, the Mongol justice system worked. It helped to keep the members of the scattered clans and tribes unified, conscious of shared community values, and civil to one another by making everyone in society subject to the same rules. The Great Yasa demonstrated that, despite his frequent brutality in war and other enterprises, Genghis Khan was at heart a remarkably enlightened ruler.

Chapter Four

Subduing Northern China

During the winter of 1206–1207 and the following spring, Genghis Khan found himself in a position far more powerful and exalted than that of any other Mongol before him. He had managed to unify the clans and tribes, a mixture of Mongolic and Turkic speakers, all with a shared nomadic culture. An unprecedented feat, this act of unification had brought at least 2 million people under his direct authority. He was not a king in the traditional sense. Historically and culturally, the Mongols did not recognize that office. And they had no crown, throne, court, or other royal trappings. Yet as khan, he was a ruler who wielded considerable, in fact almost absolute, power, as long as his people did not feel that he had abused his authority.

If the Great Khan did abuse his authority, he could expect to have his powerful position challenged. He might even be assassinated. This was because in Mongol society, as in most other ancient and medieval cultures, power-hungry individuals were always ready to take advantage of a ruler's missteps. Indeed, there was certainly no shortage of would-be khans among the Mongol elite. In addition to some strong military generals, including his own brother, Kasar, Genghis Khan had four tough sons. The eldest, Jochi, was about twenty-six when his father became Genghis Khan. Next in line came Chagatai, then about twenty-one; Ogedei was roughly twenty, and Tuli was in his teens. All were fiercely loyal to their father. But they were Mongols first. And if Genghis became corrupt and betrayed the people, family loyalty might be set aside for the greater good.

His Own Backyard

Genghis Khan was well aware of these political realities and had no intention of abusing his high office and the people's trust. The immediate question for him in

Ogedei and Jochi, two of Genghis Khan's sons, were loyal to their father but would have set aside their loyalty and overthrown him if the khan ever abused his power.

Rivalry Among Brothers

Genghis Khan's four sons were all strong and ambitious, and they sometimes argued with each other. One such argument, between Chagatai and Jochi, over whether the latter was the Great Khan's rightful heir, is recorded in *The Secret History of the Mongols*. The passage reads,

> Jochi rose up and grabbed Chagatai by the collar, saying: "I've never been set apart from my brothers by my father the Khan. What gives you the right to say that I'm different? What makes you better than I am? Maybe your heart is harder than mine. That's the only difference I can see. If you can shoot an arrow farther than I can, I'll cut off my thumb and throw it away. If you can beat me at wrestling, I'll lay still on the ground where I fall. Let the word of our father, the Khan, decide."

Paul Kahn, ed., *The Secret History of the Mongols: The Origin of Chingis Khan*, Boston: Cheng and Tsui, 1998, p. 153.

that fateful winter was what to do with the great power and authority he had amassed. True, the Mongols were united and filled with energy and eagerness to achieve major goals. But most were unsure about what those goals should be and how to accomplish them. They needed guidance and a strong leader to channel their enormous energies and help them meet their potential. Genghis Khan realized that if he did not provide that guidance, those energies might well dissipate, or even worse be misdirected into internal rivalries and civil strife.

The logical place to channel those national energies, Genghis Khan knew, was into war, more specifically conquest. Not only was he a gifted military leader, but he also had a powerful army at his command. The nomadic horsemen of the steppes were natural, exceptionally effective soldiers who had long been used to fighting among themselves. If his leadership and their skills could be properly utilized, he realized, the Mongols could potentially come to control large portions of Asia, if not all of it.

Again applying logic and reason, another of his many talents, the new Mongol ruler concluded that the best place to begin his conquests was in his own backyard. The Mongol clans lived along the borders of China. An old and venerable land, it was very populous and filled with material riches and the comforts of civilization. Conquering the Chinese would therefore hugely increase the Mongols' power, wealth, and influence,

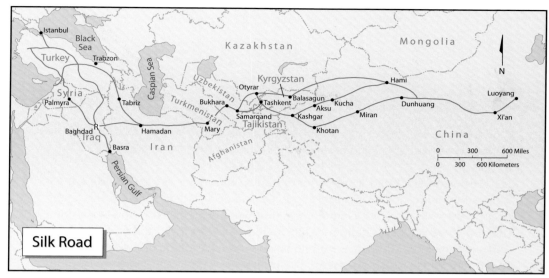

The Silk Road connected the economies of many Chinese and other central Asian cities and was the main path of business between China and the West.

all of which could then be used to overcome other peoples and nations.

Genghis Khan also realized that it would not be necessary to conquer all of China, which was enormous. At the time, it was made up of a number of political states or kingdoms that periodically fought among themselves. Of the three leading kingdoms the largest and most populous, but also the most distant from Mongolia, lay in southern China. It was ruled by the Sung dynasty (family line of rulers).

Northern China, meanwhile, which was more accessible to the Mongols, was largely divided into two large states. In the east was the Jurched (or Jurchen) kingdom, a monarchy ruled by the Jin (also Jinn or Kin) dynasty. The arrogant and aggressive Jin had taken control of the region in about 1115. These kings, who would later give rise to the Chinese

Manchus, had their royal court at Zhongdu, now the modern Chinese capital of Beijing.

Finally, in the northwest lay the kingdom of the Tangut, a people related to the Tibetans, who dwelled in the Himalayas. The southern Chinese called the Tangut the Xi-Xia. Militarily the weakest of the major Chinese peoples, the Tangut relied on the Silk Road, a major trade route that passed through their territory, for their wealth. The Silk Road not only connected and supported the economies of many Chinese and other central Asian cities, but it also kept open a small but crucial door to merchants and travelers from the Middle East and Europe. According to one modern authority,

The Silk Road was the main artery for business and trade between China and the West. It has played

East and West Exchange Innovations

The creators of an extensive modern study of the medieval Silk Road, the Silk Road Project, provide this general description of that pivotal trade network:

> The historical Silk Road was a series of trade routes that crisscrossed Eurasia for almost two-thousand years, until about the year 1500. [Over] the centuries, many important scientific and technological innovations migrated to the West along the Silk Road, including gunpowder, the magnetic compass, the printing press, silk, mathematics, [and] ceramic and lacquer crafts. Eastern and Western string, wind, and percussion instruments also traveled between regions and had strong influences on one another over time. Resources, information and innovations were exchanged between so many cultures over so many hundreds of years that it is now often difficult to identify the origins of numerous traditions that our respective cultures take for granted. In this way, the Silk Road created an intercontinental think tank of human ingenuity.

Silk Road Project, "The Silk Road," Silk Road Project, www.silkroadproject.org/education/thesilkroad/tabid/175/default.aspx.

an important role in the exchanges of cultural and trade-goods. [Chinese innovations, including the] compass and gunpowder [were] introduced to Western countries via the Silk Road. In return, many aspects of Western civilization that influenced Chinese society made their way back along this road.[42]

Submission of the Tangut

The Silk Road was undoubtedly one of the motivations for Genghis Khan's decision to make the Tangut the first target of his Chinese campaigns. Likely he reasoned that defeating the Tangut would give him control over key stretches of the Silk Road. In turn, this would bring him both wealth and a valuable overland connection to western Asian regions and peoples who might later become either his allies or his subjects.

Genghis Khan launched his invasion of the Tangut kingdom in 1207. Realizing that he and his army had no chance against the Mongols, the Tangut ruler, Burkhan Khan, surrendered and offered to become the khan's vassal, or dependent local puppet ruler. To seal the deal, Burkhan Khan also gave his daughter's

Gaining control over portions of the Silk Road, and other factors, motivated Genghis Khan to lead the Mongol conquest of China starting with the Tangut Kingdom.

hand in marriage to the Great Khan. According to the *Secret History*,

> Burkhan Khan said to him [Genghis Khan]: "I'll surrender to you and be like your right hand, giving all my strength to you." He gave Genghis Khan one of his daughters, Chakha, as a wife, and sent a message with her, saying: "When we heard tale of what Genghis Khan had done, we were afraid of him. Now that we see him before our city walls, we are afraid of his greatness and power. This fear makes us say, 'We'll be your right hand and give all our strength to you.' But when we say we'll give you all our strength, remember that we're a people whose camps don't move [like those of the Mongols], we're a people who've built city walls. Though we'll be your allies, when you go off to fight a swift campaign or quick fight, we won't be able to rush off and fight beside you. But if Genghis Khan will spare us, we Tangut will give him the camels we raise … the woolen clothing and satins we weave, [and] the best of the birds we've trained for the hunt." And Burkhan kept to this promise.[43]

Well-Conceived, Clever Tactics

Next, in 1211, Genghis Khan set his sights on conquering the Jurched. Their ruler, Xuanzong, was so wealthy that he was popularly known as the King of Gold (or Golden King). In terms of their military forces, the Jurched were considerably stronger than the Tangut. In addition to some sixty-five thousand cavalry, they had an estimated eighty-five thousand infantry, while Genghis Khan's army also had sixty-five thousand horsemen but possessed virtually no foot soldiers.

However, the Mongol leader had an important advantage. Namely, his troops were more logically and effectively deployed, both on and off the battlefield. For example, like almost all other ancient and medieval armies, the Jurched soldiers marched along in columns with their food and other supplies behind them in a cumbersome baggage train. Such formations were slow moving and easy targets for enemy ambushes. In contrast, each Mongol horseman carried what he needed himself. Also, the traveling fighters spread out over a large area. That way they could more easily avoid enemy patrols and find pastures for their animals, as well as move swiftly toward their destination—either the battlefield or the next campsite. In addition, the marching camps for all Mongol regiments or other large groups were

Genghis Khan deployed his troops more effectively both on and off the battlefield, often giving him and his troops the advantage to win a battle.

laid out in identical fashion. That way, as the soldiers reported in from various directions, they knew exactly where to set up their tents, where the officers were stationed, and so forth.

Other potent advantages for Genghis Khan and his forces were the well-conceived strategy and clever tactics he devised to defeat the Jurcheds. One tactic was to use the large numbers of Chinese peasant farmers in the King of Gold's realm against him. First, units of Mongol horsemen attacked and torched peasant villages, which were small and largely undefended. As their homes and crops burned, the terrified farmers swarmed onto the roads, which became clogged, slowing down Jurched messengers and relief troops. Hundreds of thousands of peasants also flooded into nearby cities. There they consumed vast stores of food that the Jurched leaders needed to feed their families and soldiers. The Mongols also used large groups of local refugees as human shields by placing them in front of their advancing cavalry units, so that Jurched soldiers hesitated to fire for fear of killing their own people.

Genghis Khan displayed other effective tactics designed to allow him to capture walled enemy cities quickly and with very minimal loss of his own troops. In one incident, the Mongols were besieging the Jurched city of Dading. After they captured a messenger the King of Gold had sent to the city, one of Khan's own men dressed in the envoy's clothes, took his official papers, and continued on to the city. A few hours later, following Genghis Khan's plan, the Mongols packed up and departed. The fake envoy then proceeded to convince the city's leaders that the Mongols had given up the siege. It was now safe to dismantle the city's elaborate defenses, he said, and the leaders, believing him, complied. A week or two later, however, the disguised Mongol sent word to his master, the khan, who suddenly returned with his forces and easily captured the now unprotected city.

The colorful story of Khan's capture of another Jurched city may or may not be based in fact. Some modern scholars think Genghis Khan himself invented it and circulated it among the enemy population to make them believe he was far too clever for their leader, the King of Gold, to defeat. Scholar Peter Brent summarizes the famous story:

> He now informed the commander of the fortified town that he would lead his men home if he received [from the city's leaders] one thousand cats and ten thousand swallows. One imagines the startled debate within the walls. [Eventually] the curious payment was made. Now the Khan set his Mongols to work, tying tufts of cottonwood to the tails of these beasts, setting [fire] to them and letting them go in one terrified, flickering stampede through air and over land. Like sparks blown by a gale, birds searched for their nests, cats for their haunts. Beyond the [city's] walls, smoke arose, first here, then there, soon in a dozen places, in a hundred, [and] the whole town blazed.[44]

Learning to Use Catapults

At first the Mongols knew nothing about siege warfare. But as Genghis Khan was invading China, he realized he needed to learn this aspect of war as quickly as possible. According to a team of University of Calgary scholars led by Christon I. Archer,

> Genghis [Khan] conscripted Chinese craftsmen and engineers, who showed the Mongols how to operate the light Chinese-type catapult, which required forty men to pull back the ropes connected to the wooden arm under tension, while the heavy [Chinese] catapult required one hundred men. These catapults had limited ranges of 100 to 150 yards, and their missiles were small, ranging from two to twenty-five pounds. However, after the fall of Samarkand in 1220, Persian and Middle Eastern catapults were copied, meaning that the catapult operated via a counterweight, like the western trebuchet, and longer distances and heavier stones could be used. ... Later, under the khan Mongke in 1252, all Chinese metal workers, carpenters, and gunpowder makers were registered as catapult operators, and these formed the basis of the one thousand catapult crews who accompanied the Mongol armies to Persia in 1253.

Genghis Khan enlisted Chinese craftsmen and engineers to show the Mongols how to use siege warfare, specifically the catapult.

Christon I. Archer et al., *World History of Warfare*, Lincoln: University of Nebraska Press, 2002, p. 178.

While the city's guards and soldiers desperately fought the flames, the Mongols swooped down on the burning city and captured it with minimal effort.

The Battle of Beijing

Not all of the cities Genghis Khan captured fell because of such stealth tactics. He also set about learning the art of traditional siege warfare, in part by capturing Chinese engineers and persuading them to teach him. These men (and later several Persian engineers as well) also built a number of large siege devices for him. They included catapults that hurled stones at or over city walls; the trebuchet, a device similar to a gigantic sling, which flung rocks even farther than a catapult could; and the ballista, essentially a big crossbow that shot huge arrowlike bolts. Although the Mongols knew nothing about these machines at first, they swiftly became adept at operating them.

Eventually, the Great Khan felt confident enough to lay siege to the Jurched capital of Zhongdu. This promised to be no easy task, for modern experts estimate it then had at least 225,000 houses and about a million inhabitants. Moreover, it was extremely well defended. Nevertheless, in 1214 the determined Mongol leader ordered his men to surround the city and prepared to do whatever was necessary to capture it. (In later ages, after the city's name changed from Zhongdu to Beijing, the Chinese somewhat inaccurately came to call the siege the Battle of Beijing.)

The King of Gold, Xuanzong, at first hoped to outlast the besiegers. But as time went on, his military advisers warned him that the Mongols would not give up and would eventually overrun the city. According to the *Secret History*, a trusted general told the king:

Destiny is with the Mongols. Heaven and Earth are on their side [and] the Mongol army is so powerful they've killed the finest and most courageous soldiers of China [and] slaughtered so many [that] our army's destroyed. ... I say we should offer tribute [payment acknowledging submission] to the Khan of the Mongols for now, and negotiate some settlement with him.[45]

Xuanzong agreed with what his general had said and reluctantly decided to make a deal with Genghis Khan. According to the *Secret History*,

He sent a message offering tribute to Genghis Khan, and gave him one of his daughters as a wife. The gates of Zhongdu were opened and they [the Jurched] set out great quantities of gold, silver, satins, and other goods, letting the men of the Mongol army divide it themselves, depending on how many beasts each had to carry the load. [The king's general, Fu-hsing] went to negotiate with Genghis Khan, and Genghis agreed to talk with him, accepting their tribute, and ordered his men to stop fighting and return from all the towns they had taken. The [Mongol] army withdrew to the north.[46]

This episode, among other similar ones, once more showed the Great Khan was a reasonable man if presented with a situation that favored both his own side and the enemy's. And it appears that one of the greatest cities of the medieval world would have been spared if the King of Gold had kept his side of the bargain. However, he did not. Once the Mongols had withdrawn, he decided to get as far away from the Mongols as he could. Xuanzong, his family, his generals, and his leading courtiers fled southward to the city of Kaifeng. There, they hoped to be out of reach of the Great Khan.

In this, the Jurched ruler was quite wrong. On hearing of Xuanzong's treachery, Genghis Khan was livid and began to muster his forces. As Khan and his army entered China once more, large numbers of Jurched Chinese, soldiers and peasants alike, joined his cause. The new recruits were persuaded by the Great Khan's stark "either/or" choice. Either the people join his cause and live or oppose him and be destroyed.

Other allies from the regions north of China also arrived to help the Mongols. Reaching the capital in June 1215, these allies ransacked and looted it. Then, large numbers of Mongol troops moved out into the surrounding farmland, where they trampled large tracts of crops under their horses' hooves. The aim of this tactic was twofold—to deprive the enemy of needed foodstuffs and to turn the plowed farmland back into pastures that could be used for grazing by Mongol horses, cattle, and other livestock.

A Desire for More

This second foray into the Jurched-ruled sector of China was intended to be much more than punishment and retaliation for the King of Gold's rebellion. It was also an opportunity to enrich the Mongol soldiers and civilians. When the campaign was over, Genghis Khan brought thousands of tons of Chinese goods back to the Mongolian camps on the steppes. Caravan after caravan, each with hundreds of carts, carried bolts of silk and other fine fabrics, tapestries and wall-hangings, furniture, dinnerware, rugs, pillows, blankets, brass cooking pots, iron kettles, saddles, bronze knives, casks of wine, jugs of perfume, board games, bales of tea, jars of spices, suits of metal armor, and much more.

This was only the beginning of an immense inflow of products from foreign lands that would persist as long as Genghis Khan's conquests continued. Throughout these years, most Mongols would go on living in makeshift tents, as their ancestors had. But those dwellings often became larger and more comfortable, and in some cases even luxurious.

Because the Mongols had been unused to such extravagances in the past, the sudden availability of these products changed not only their lifestyle but also their attitudes about owning material things. As has happened in numerous other societies both before and after that time, having more than they were used to inspired a desire for still more. "Novelties became necessities," as one expert explains, "and each caravan of cargo stimulated a craving for more. The more he conquered, the more he *had* to conquer."[47]

Another unexpected outcome of acquiring so much newfound wealth was the problem of where to store the excess. So much loot flowed into the Mongol heartland that there was not enough room for it all in the people's houses. The solution was to build permanent storage facilities, which had never before existed in their society. Along with the mountains of goods, the army shipped in many foreign artisans and builders, who showed Khan's people how to erect structures where the excess could be safely kept.

"A Liberty of Conscience"

The influx of Chinese artisans and other foreigners into Mongol society exposed the Mongols and their leader to new social and religious ideas. The time the Mongols spent in foreign cities and countries while conquering and occupying them also exposed them to new ideas. As a result, over time at least some Mongols converted to other faiths.

These religious conversions posed no political problem, mainly because of Genghis Khan's attitude and policies regarding religion, which the peoples the Mongols encountered found unusual, even remarkable. The khan, who had an open and quite sophisticated toleration for any and all belief systems, granted complete religious freedom to all the peoples he conquered. He even gave tax exemptions to their churches, mosques, and temples. Scholar J.J. Saunders explains,

Christians, Muslims, Jews, [and] Buddhists, all acquired perfect liberty to worship as they pleased and to propagate [spread] their tenets [ideas] anywhere in the Mongol realm, provided they did not encroach on the freedom of others. Never had the continent of Asia enjoyed so complete a liberty of conscience, never had it been filled with so many ardent missionaries seeking to push their doctrines. Thus, the clergy of all competing religions tended to preach loyalty to the Mongols, a circumstance which helped to perpetuate their rule.[48]

Genghis Khan's policy of religious toleration was so sweeping and sophisticated, in fact, that not until modern times, with the advent of open democracies like the United States, was it seen again.

When foreigners praised the Great Khan for his wisdom in adopting such enlightened attitudes toward religion, he usually reacted with modesty. He was only a humble man with limited abilities, he claimed, who had been thrust into an important position of responsibility and special destiny. "I hate luxury and exercise moderation," he said.

I have only one coat and one food. I eat the same food and am dressed in the same tatters as my humble herdsmen. ... I have not myself distinguished qualities, [but] as my calling is high, the obligations incumbent on [expected of] me are also heavy and I fear that in my rule there may be something wanting.[49]

In retrospect, however, considering the khan's deeds and statements as a whole, modern experts see this as false modesty. The truth is that Genghis Khan knew full well that he was anything but ordinary. In fact, he felt that the great god Tengri had endowed him with special abilities and a singular destiny—to rule the known world. The proof of this is that as soon as he had secured the Chinese territories he had overrun, he turned his armies westward, intent on bringing the vast Middle East into the Mongol fold.

Chapter Five

Conquests in Western Asia

After conquering northern China and gaining control of much of central Asia, Genghis Khan was extremely powerful and wealthy. He had also made sure to pass on much of the loot he had captured in war to his people. However, he knew that there were many more riches to be had in western Asia. The Silk Road continued into the region, which was crisscrossed by several other lucrative trade routes. If he could tap into that trade, the Mongol realm could conceivably become the wealthiest state in all of Asia.

The Failed Peace Offer

Early in 1218 Genghis Khan sent a letter, accompanied by several cart loads of expensive gifts, to Muhammad II, ruler of the Khwarezmid Empire, or Khwarizm. This enormous Muslim-controlled realm encompassed most of Persia (present-day Iran), Afghanistan, and Transoxiana (the region lying east of the Caspian Sea near modern-day Uzbekistan and Tajikistan). In sheer numbers of soldiers and support personnel, it was then the strongest military power in Asia. It was also very wealthy thanks to the trade routes that passed through it.

When Muhammad, who held the exalted title of Khwarizm shah, or sultan, read the letter, he saw that Genghis Khan was offering peace. "I am the sovereign of the sunrise," the letter stated, "and you the sovereign of the sunset."[50] The khan went on to say that he already controlled huge amounts of territory. So he had no need to launch conquests against Khwarizm. Instead, he desired to forge a friendship with Muhammad and to initiate trade between the two empires so that both would benefit. The shah sent back word that he accepted the khan's offer. But later events show that, for reasons of his own, Muhammad was not sincere and planned to turn on the Mongol leader.

Thinking he had made a solid, good-faith deal, Genghis Khan gathered together some 450 Muslim and Hindu merchants who lived in his realm. He loaded them down with silk, jade, silver, and other valuable commodities and ordered them to travel to Khwarizm and give these gifts to the shah. Not long after the merchants entered Khwarezmid territory, however, a local governor killed them and seized the goods. The governor had no idea that this act was destined to set into motion the terrifying wrath of the Mongol hordes. As Persian historian Ata-Malik Juvaini explains, in depriving "these men of their lives and possessions," the governor "desolated and laid waste a whole world and rendered a whole creation without home, property or leaders."[51]

Hearing what had happened to the merchants, Genghis Khan was, not surprisingly, furious. He sent three envoys to the shah to demand that the governor who had slain the merchants be turned over to the Mongols for punishment. In a reaction no less arrogant and unwise than the governor's, the shah killed one

Genghis Khan's Temper

Genghis Khan was known to have a bad temper when things did not go his way. Proof of this includes an incident that occurred while he and his sons were campaigning in the western Asian region of Persia. According to *The Secret History of the Mongols*,

> When Jochi, Chagadai, and Ogedei took the city of Gurganj, they divided the city's people [and their loot] three ways and didn't leave a part for Genghis Khan. Genghis Khan yelled at the three of them [and] for three days he wouldn't see them. Then his three commanders … petitioned him, saying, "We've made the Muslim sultan bow at our feet. [Why] has the Khan grown angry? Your sons know what they've done wrong but now they're afraid of your anger. If you continue this way you'll break their spirits. Let them come see you face to face."

Khan agreed to see his sons and, after he had yelled loudly at them a second time, his anger cooled and he began preparing for the next campaign.

Paul Kahn, ed., *The Secret History of the Mongols: The Origin of Chingis Khan*, Boston: Cheng and Tsui, 1998, p. 159.

of the envoys. Then he burned the beards off the faces of the other two and sent them back to Khan with a message of mockery and defiance. At this disrespectful rebuke, Genghis Khan was even more enraged than before. According to Juvaini,

> These tidings had such an effect on the Khan's mind that the control of repose and tranquility was removed, and the whirlwind of anger cast dust into the eyes of patience and clemency while the fire of wrath flared up with such a flame that it drove the water from his eyes and could be quenched only by the shedding of blood.[52]

The Empire's Shaky Foundations

As he prepared for war against Khwarizm, the Mongol ruler made sure, as he had in the past, to gather as much intelligence, or useful information about the enemy, as possible. Questioning merchants and others, he learned that Muhammad's empire was a fairly new one. It had formed only a little more than a decade before his own. Moreover, in addition to being large—it stretched from west-central Asia into the Middle East—it had a huge and diverse population. Included were Arabic, Turkic, Persian, and other speakers. There were also numerous minority faiths, among them Christianity, Judaism, and Zoroastrianism (Old Persian), in addition to Islam, the religion of the ruling classes. Frequent tensions and rivalries existed among these linguistic and religious groups. In fact, even the realm's Muslims were divided into factions that did not get along.

What is more, Muhammad had been unable to end these divisions because he lacked the talent and wisdom to rule effectively. "Vain, frivolous, and incompetent," one modern scholar remarks, he "was neither a statesman nor a soldier, and his soaring ambition to reign [a mighty kingdom] was belied by his clear unfitness for the role. To him must be ascribed much of the blame for the hideous calamities which [followed]."[53]

For these reasons, Genghis Khan came to realize, the Khwarezmid Empire was actually considerably weaker than it appeared on surface. This would work to his advantage, he decided, as he began to devise his strategy for the upcoming campaign. One part of the plan was, when possible, to break down the Mongol army into separate units and attack from two or more directions at once. This approach was designed to make it look like Khan had larger forces than he actually did. Another successful tactic was to fabricate letters from Muhammad's leading nobles and send them to the shah. These forgeries gave that leader the impression that his nobles were on the verge of deserting him. Genghis Khan also sent messengers to numerous Khwarezmid villages to remind the inhabitants about the shah's heavy taxes and poor leadership. These shrewd moves further weakened an empire that was already resting on shaky foundations.

Late in 1218, the Great Khan's forces moved westward for what proved to be

CONQUÊTES DE GENGIS-KAN.

Although mercenary armies fighting for the Khwarezmid Empire outnumbered the Mongol horsemen and their Chinese allies, ethnic and religious tensions between the hired mercenaries nullified the Khwarezmid Empire's numerical advantage.

a date with destiny. The total army consisted of 110,000 to 125,000 Mongol horsemen and another 60,000 or more Chinese and other allies. The shah was able to muster much larger forces, numbering 400,000 or more. However, many of these were mercenaries (paid fighters) who felt little or no loyalty to their commanders. Further weakening the army's ranks were ethnic and religious tensions among soldiers from various sectors of the empire. These factors more than nullified the significant numerical advantage the Khwarezmid forces enjoyed.

"The Punishment of God"

As they approached the eastern border of Muhammad's realm early in 1219, the Mongols split up into three groups, following Genghis Khan's plan. Genghis Khan's sons, Ogedei and Chagatai, attacked the city of Otrar, situated east of the Aral Sea. The Mongol general Jebe (or Chepe) led a second group on a more southerly route. Finally, the Great Khan himself commanded the primary attack force, which moved through the Kizil Kum desert, northwest of Otrar. The common wisdom was that no army could successfully cross this vast wasteland. So when the khan and his men emerged from the desert north of the important Khwarezmid city of Bukhara, the residents were taken completely by surprise.

Swooping down on the city, the Mongols easily overcame the soldiers guarding it. They then entered and killed several thousand of its thirty thousand inhabitants. The attackers then herded close to three hundred of the leading citizens into a large mosque. As the terrified people gazed toward the front, they saw an imposing, well-armed man appear and mount the pulpit. Some likely guessed correctly that he was the renowned Mongol leader himself. "O people," he told them in a stern voice, "know that you have committed great sins." The proof for this charge was simple, he told them. "I am the punishment of God. If you had not committed great sins, God would not have sent a punishment like me upon you."[54] He then sent the citizens out, each accompanied by a Mongol soldier, to gather up their valuables and bring them to a central location, where his carts were waiting.

Soon afterward, the Mongols burned Bukhara and moved on to the Khwarezmid capital of Samarkand, lying several miles to the southeast. The large, populous city had strong walls and was heavily guarded. But it took the Mongols only ten days to capture it, after which they fanned out across the empire, destroying towns and massacring large numbers of people as they went. One common tactic was to kill most or all of the aristocrats and other upper-class people in each city. That, the reasoning went, would eliminate most of the local leaders who might later organize rebellions against the Mongols.

The Benefits of Renewal

The Mongol conquest of Khwarizm, followed by its revolution, demonstrated that, no matter how destructive the Mongols were during their military campaigns, they always looked ahead to rebuilding and the political, administrative, and cultural rewards that came from it. In particular, they knew that such renewal encouraged trade, which was essential to their economic well-being. According to scholar J.J. Saunders,

> Their material interest was never lost sight of. [No matter how] merciless their rage for destruction, they commonly permitted, after a decent interval, the rebuilding of the cities they had burned and ruined, since they were satisfied that ruins produced no revenue [or] flourishing trade.

J.J. Saunders, *The History of the Mongol Conquests*, Philadelphia: University of Pennsylvania Press, 2001, p. 56.

The destruction was so widespread that Khwarizm was almost wiped from the face of the earth and much of the region remained devastated for centuries afterward. Eighteenth-century English historian Edward Gibbon remarked: "From the Caspian to the Indus [River], they [the Mongols] ruined a tract of many hundred[s of] miles, which was adorned with the habitations and labors of mankind, [and] five centuries have not been sufficient to repair the ravages of four years."[55]

During the conquest of Khwarizm by the Mongols, one of history's most remarkable examples of military aggression, adventure, and sheer boldness occurred. As his empire crumbled around him, Shah Muhammad fled northwestward to the shores of the Caspian. Genghis Khan's trusted generals Subodei and Jebe gathered about twenty thousand troops and gave chase, intent on bringing the enemy leader back alive if possible. The shah ended up dying on an island in the Caspian. But Subodei, Jebe, and their men, with the Great Khan's blessing, continued northward along the shore of that immense waterway. In the next three years they covered an incredible 8,000 miles (12,875km), entirely circling the sea and even reaching the shores of the Black Sea. Gibbon later called it "an expedition which had never been attempted, and has never been repeated."[56]

Along the way, the wayward Mongols passed through one nation after another. They also met numerous armies in battle, including a force of some eighty

After attacking the city of Bukhara, Genghis Khan sent the citizens out—each accompanied by a Mongol soldier—to bring back their valuables to load in his carts.

thousand Russians commanded by the prince of the city of Kiev. Amazingly, the two capable and unrelenting Mongol generals defeated this enormous throng and eventually made it back to Persia, where they rejoined the Great Khan. This bold venture proved important because it gave the Mongols a glimpse of what lay farther to the west—the fertile steppes of Russia and beyond them eastern Europe. The "astonishing raid," scholar J.J. Saunders writes, "which defeated twenty nations and achieved a complete circuit of the Caspian … set a precedent for the invasion of eastern Europe nearly twenty years later."[57]

Economic and Administrative Reforms

By the time Subodei and Jebe made it back to what had once been the Khwarezmid Empire, they found their boss hard at work reshaping the region to make it a more manageable part of his own realm. A few of the cities he had burned were already partially rebuilt. Others, however, were not only left in ruins, but their very foundations were also dug up, broken up, and covered over with dirt. The Great Khan also moved through the countryside, ordering the residents of some villages and towns to abandon their homes and rebuild elsewhere.

There were two principal reasons for this wholesale reordering and relocation of towns and local populations. First, Genghis Khan wanted to create large new areas of grasslands where few or none had existed for many centuries. Scholar Jack Weatherford explains,

He depopulated expansive areas of land [and when] the villagers and farmers left, [the] fields reverted to grazing land. This allowed large areas to be set aside for the herds [of horses] that accompanied the army and were kept as reserves for future campaigns. Just as when he churned up the agricultural land when he left northern China, [Genghis Khan] always wanted a clear area of retreat or advancement where his

army could always find adequate pasturage for the horses and for the other animals on which their success depended.[58]

The second reason that Khan endeavored to eradicate some towns, move others, and build some new ones was that he wanted to realign the main trade routes passing through the region. He felt that doing so would make it easier for his governors and other officials to control them. As had always been the case, he fully recognized the importance of having a strong, bustling economy that produced as much revenue as possible. Among other things, this required trade goods to flow unimpeded through the territories making up his empire. Indeed, Saunders says,

Everything was done to encourage a brisk commercial traffic. The roads were policed, post-houses [rest stops and inns] established, caravans given armed protection, [and] thieves and robbers put down. The peasants tilling their fields in the fertile oases of central Asia were guarded against the old curse of peaceful cultivators—raids by nomadic tribes. Mongol military power, perhaps we may add Mongol terror [tactics], made the highways of Asia safer than they had ever been. Companies of merchants who entered partnership with a prince [local leader] who provided the capital [financial backing] were given extensive rights and privileges, including exemption from direct taxation, and they journeyed regularly to and fro across the continent from China to Persia and beyond. [Thus] when a region was subjugated [by the Mongols], Genghis Khan took care to put its economy on a new footing. [Selected] ruined cities were rebuilt, and the trading classes [were] encouraged to resume their operation under the protection of the Mongol army. Profits must have been high and the influential moneyed men were long among the strongest props of the Mongol Empire.[59]

To help support and perpetuate this sound financial organization, Khan also put into place a well-ordered, practical administrative apparatus. He chose skilled, trusted men to run the cities and provinces of the now defunct Khwarezmid realm. These officials were expected to collect taxes from the local inhabitants and make sure the accumulated money or goods made it back to the Mongolian heartland intact.

The administrators also oversaw public works. This included not only building and maintaining structures in towns, but also making sure that mounted messengers and rest stops for them were always in operation. That way the khan's orders, as well as news about various sectors of the empire, could travel as quickly as possible.

In addition, the local officials chosen by the khan had the task of levying troops from their territories when Mongol generals needed them. Some of these

soldiers guarded the towns. This reasonably inexpensive practice was so effective that it paid for itself many times over. The fact was that the presence of even small numbers of Mongol warriors in a given area was a potent deterrent to rebellion and corruption there.

The Matter of the Succession

When he was satisfied that his new imperial lands in western Asia had been put into good running order, Genghis Khan, now almost sixty, headed back to

This illustration shows Genghis Khan and his soldiers storming a Tangut fortress. Khan's second attack against the Tangut caused him injuries which later led to his death.

Mongolia. It was at about this time that he chose a successor in the event that he died. Sixty was considered to be fairly old in a world in which average life expectancy was not much over thirty. Although Khan hoped he had many years left, he realistically faced the fact that he might meet his end unexpectedly at any moment. After much thought and soul-searching, he selected his third son, Ogedei, to be the next Great Khan. True, as the oldest, Jochi technically had seniority. But after the sons met and discussed the matter, they agreed, probably reluctantly on the parts of Jochi and Chagatai, that Ogedei had the best skills and personality for the position. So the entire family backed Genghis Khan's decision.

As it turned out, it was fortunate for the family, and the Mongols as a whole, that the matter of succession was resolved at that time. On returning to his homeland, Genghis Khan learned that the Tangut, whom he had defeated years before, had become troublesome. Their leader, Burkhan Khan, was no longer living up to all the terms of the agreement he had earlier made with the Mongols. So in 1226, Genghis Khan once more led his soldiers against the Tangut.

This turned out to be the Mongol leader's last campaign. In its midst, he was thrown from his horse and suffered

Four Brothers United

English historian Edward Gibbon, author of *Decline and Fall of the Roman Empire*, said the following about Genghis Khan's sons, among whom Ogedei became the heir to the office of Great Khan:

Of his numerous progeny [children], four sons, illustrious by their birth and merit, exercised under their father the principal offices of peace and war. Jochi was his great huntsman, Chagatai his judge, Ogedei his minister [administrator], and Tuli his general. And their names and actions are often conspicuous in the history of his conquests. Firmly united for their own and the public interest, [the] brothers and their families were content with dependent [positions of power]. And Ogedei, by general consent, was proclaimed Great Khan, or emperor, [after Genghis Khan's death].

Edward Gibbon, *The Decline and Fall of the Roman Empire*, vol. 3, ed. David Womersley, New York: Penguin, 1994, p. 798.

Toute puissance est faible, à moins que d'être unie.
LA FONTAINE.

In the summer of 1227, after being bedridden for months, Genghis Khan passed away.

some serious internal injuries. Both his doctors and generals begged him to retire to the steppes and take a long rest. But he refused. He continued to manage the operations against the Tangut, and in the spring of 1227 their capital fell. At that point, while still in considerable pain from his recent injuries, Genghis Khan contracted a grave illness. Exactly what it was remains unclear, but the best guess of modern medical experts is either malaria or typhus. After that, he was bedridden for a few months. Finally, in the late summer of 1227 he passed away at the age of sixty-five (or somewhat younger, depending on which of the estimates of his birth year one accepts).

According to the *Secret History*, "Genghis Khan ascended into Heaven."[60] However, his surviving enemies were undoubtedly sure that he had gone in the opposite direction. Whatever the fate of his soul, no one could argue about the results of his accomplishments. At that moment, the imperial realm he had created stretched from eastern China westward across Asia to Persia. Already one of history's largest land empires, it was about to become *the* largest, for his successors proved to be no less ambitious than he had been.

Chapter Six

The Mongols After Genghis Khan

The death of Genghis Khan was a tremendous emotional blow to the Mongols, for they had regarded him as a leader sent and supported by their great god Tengri. There were no worries or disputes about who would succeed him, however. Ogedei had already been chosen by his father to become the new Great Khan after his death. Thus, the transfer of power went smoothly, as Ogedei immediately assumed authority in 1227 and the Mongols officially proclaimed him their ruler two years later. He and his own successors were destined to bring the Mongol Empire to its zenith. Almost as quickly, though, they would allow it to fall into division and decline, the fate of all empires in human history.

The Assault on Europe

As khan, Ogedei was a vigorous leader who initiated a number of ambitious projects in the 1230s. One that rapidly achieved completion was the creation of a new, permanent Mongol capital at Karakorum, in central Mongolia. Ogedei also launched invasions of southern China, still ruled by the Sung dynasts, and Korea, lying east of China.

One of the new khan's biggest, most daring endeavors was an attempt to extend the empire's western boundaries into Russia and even beyond. At his orders, Batu, Jochi's son, and the widely respected Mongol general Subodei attacked the Bulgars, Alans, and other peoples who lived on the Russian steppes. The campaign was highly successful and ended in 1240 with the fall of the region's major city of Kiev.

Mongol successes in Russia left the way open for an incursion into eastern Europe. The invaders swept through what is now Hungary while a group of eastern European dukes and princes hastily formed a coalition to try to meet the threat. The big showdown came in

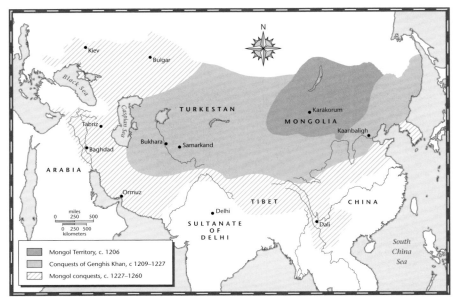

Genghis Khan's successor, his son Ogedei, created the permanent Mongol capital at Karakorum and launched invasions of China and Korea to expand the empire.

April 1241 at Liegnitz, in Poland. The European commanders, among them Duke Henry II of the Polish realm of Silesia, swiftly fell prey to Mongol stealth tactics, for which they were woefully unprepared. University of Swansea scholar John France recalls,

> Duke Henry, seeing what he thought was a small enemy army, sent his cavalry forward against their center, but the wings of the Mongol army [which had been hidden from view] now revealed themselves and swept around the attacking knights, separating them from the rest of their army. Accounts refer to the Mongols using smoke to confuse the westerners and this may be true, since gunpowder was known to the Mongols

from China. Duke Henry was killed in the rout of his army and most of his troops were slaughtered. The Mongols cut off ears to count enemy dead and after Liegnitz are said to have sent home nine bags full of this gory evidence.[61]

With the eastern European alliance shattered by the invaders, there seemed little hope for the rest of Europe. Early in December 1241 Batu and Subodei pushed on, crossed the Danube River and advanced on the major European city of Vienna. Yet, suddenly, as quickly as the Mongol menace had appeared, it receded. According to scholar Frank E. Smitha,

> Mysteriously to Europeans, the Mongols [abruptly] retreated from

In April 1241, Mongol forces worked their way west into Europe. Ogedei's death in December, however, resulted in the withdrawl of Mongol troops from Europe.

central Europe. To the Europeans it seemed they had been saved by a miracle. A myth was to rise among the Poles that their brave warriors saved Europe from the Mongols. In reality, the Mongol withdrawal was in response to Ogedei's death, on December 11. High ranking Mongol army leaders believed they had to return to confirm the selecting of a new ruler.[62]

Mongke and Hulegu

Batu was particularly worried about the royal succession. He seems to have felt that, as the son of Jochi, Genghis Khan's eldest son, he was rightfully the next Great Khan. But when Batu reached Mongolia, he was in for a rude awakening. Rumors had long circulated that Jochi was the son of a Mongol who had impregnated his mother before she had married Genghis Khan. Whether or not this was actually the case, a number of Mongol leaders worried that Jochi and, therefore, Batu might not be directly related to Genghis Khan. Uncomfortable about electing Batu their supreme leader, they instead chose Ogedei's son, Guyuk. Because Guyuk was too young to rule, his mother, Ogedei's widow Toregene, briefly administered the realm as regent.

Guyuk took charge in the mid-1240s, but he died prematurely in 1248, leaving the position of Great Khan unfilled once more. This time a civil war broke out to decide the succession. Although ineligible to become khan, Batu was still highly influential. He supported his cousin, Mongke, the son of Tuli, Genghis Khan's fourth and youngest son. Mongke won the struggle and became Great Khan in 1251. Soon after taking power, he announced that he intended to continue the conquest of the Sung Chinese, which Ogedei had begun.

Mongke himself took charge of the operations in southern China. In the meantime, he sent his brother, Hulegu, to solidify Mongol rule in Persia and to initiate the conquest of Mesopotamia (now Iraq) and its capital of Baghdad, lying west of Persia. Hulegu marched westward across Asia at the head of a large army. In addition to the usual Mongol cavalry and selected Asian allies, the force contained many formidable siege weapons.

Hulegu's first order of business on reaching Persia was to find and eradicate a Muslim group that later came to be called the Assassins (from which the term *assassin* derives). The members of the group had been murdering local rulers, causing political difficulties and spreading fear throughout the region. In fairly short order, Hulegu and his men hunted down the Assassins, including their leader, the so-called Grand Master. Thereafter these professional killers, who had finally met their match

In the 1250s Genghis Khan's grandsons, Mongke and Hulegu, continued the expansion of the Mongol Empire.

Ogedei's Message of Compassion

Having inherited his father's position after Genghis Khan's death, Ogedei Khan tried to show that he was a thoughtful ruler who was interested in his people's welfare. He issued a public message of compassion for those subjects who were in need, saying in part,

> Let all my subjects live in peace and happiness, with their feet on the ground, with their hands on the earth. While I rule, no member of this Nation established by Genghis Khan will lack shelter or food ... no one will go hungry for their daily broth. Let every person set aside one two-year-old [male sheep] from their flocks, and one yearling sheep for every hundred in his flock. Let every person set these aside year after year and give them to the poor and needy members of their units. ... Let the thousands of mares be brought in from all directions and be milked by their herders. After they're milked ... the milk will be distributed to everyone.

Quoted in Paul Kahn, ed., *The Secret History of the Mongols: The Origin of Chingis Khan*, Boston: Cheng and Tsui, 1998, p. 173.

in the Mongols, disappeared from the pages of history.

Next, Hulegu entered Mesopotamia and in February 1258 laid siege to Baghdad. The Caliph of Baghdad, who had underestimated the invaders, was unable to mount a credible defense, so the city fell in only a week. The Mongols slaughtered many of the inhabitants, confiscated the caliph's treasures, and destroyed numerous buildings. What had been the finest city in the Middle East—a famous center of culture, literature, and the arts—was destroyed. This proved a devastating blow to Muslim civilization in the region, which did not begin to recover until modern times.

The Reign of Kublai Khan

Hulegu may well have gone on to conquer other lands lying farther to the west. But once again the sudden death of a khan intervened and changed the course of history. In 1259 Mongke Khan died while attacking the Sung Chinese, terminating the campaign and prompting other Mongol leaders to end their own operations. Thus, Hulegu never made any further conquests. He did, however, quite wisely hold onto what he had already captured. In the years to come, he set up his own separate, personal Mongol realm, or khanate, which centered in Persia, became known as the Il-khanate.

Meanwhile, events occurring back in Mongolia further demonstrated that Mongke's death marked the end of true Mongol unity. After his passing, two of his and Hulegu's other brothers, Kublai (or Qubilai) and Ariq Buqa, were both elected Great Khan by rival factions of Mongol soldiers. This resulted in a bloody power struggle. It was not until 1264 that Kublai emerged as the victor in the civil war and the undisputed Great Khan. His empire stretched from China in the east to Mesopotamia in the west and marked the greatest historical extent of Mongol territory. It was during his legendary reign, in which he supported the arts and other cultural pursuits, that European traveler Marco Polo visited central and eastern Asia. (Polo's later writings, which have survived, paint a vivid picture of Mongol society at the time.)

However, although Mongols everywhere recognized Kublai Khan as their leader, multiple Mongol power centers, the khanates, were already taking shape. Kublai ruled from northern China and was mostly concerned with events and policies centered there and in nearby areas. As time went on, and especially after his death, the leaders of the other khanates came to decide the policies and fates of their own regions. For example, Hulegu Khan and his son, Abaqa (who succeeded him after his death in 1265), tended to affairs in Persia and

Marco Polo, pictured kneeling before Kubilai Khan, visited central and eastern Asia during Kubilai's reign.

An Eyewitness Describes Kublai Khan

In his writings, Marco Polo describes Kublai, or Kubilai, Khan and his royal court, along with Mongol society. Polo says this about the Great Khan's physical attributes and his leading wives:

> Let me tell you next of the personal appearance of the Great Lord of Lords whose name is Kubilai Khan. He is a man of good stature, neither short nor tall, but of moderate height. His limbs are well fleshed out and modeled in due proportion. His complexion is fair and ruddy like a rose, the eyes black and handsome, the nose shapely and set squarely in place. He has four consorts who are all accounted his lawful wives. And his eldest son by any of these four has a rightful claim to be the emperor on the death of the present Khan. They are called empresses, each by her own name. Each of these ladies holds her own court. None of them has less than 300 ladies in waiting, all of great beauty and charm. [Each] one of these ladies has in her court 10,000 persons.

Marco Polo, *The Travels of Marco Polo*, New York: Orion Press, n.d., p. 92.

surrounding lands and had no part in Kublai's wars in the east.

From his position in the north, Kublai marshaled his energies for a new invasion of Sung-ruled southern China. In 1268 his naval forces were successful in operations along the Han River, a tributary of the Yangtze River. During the decade that followed, several major land victories and another naval win, along with the capture of the southern Chinese capital of Guangzhou, brought the Sung to their knees.

During these long and arduous campaigns, Kublai Khan also busied himself with administrative and other reforms. One of the most ambitious and important

was moving his capital from Karakorum to Zhongdu (modern Beijing), which he renamed Tatu (or Dadu). Not long afterward, he also established a summer capital and retreat several miles to the north at Shangdu, which in early modern European literature was immortalized as Xanadu (pronounced ZAN-uh-doo).

Another of Kublai's major military ventures consisted of two attempts to invade Japan. In the late 1260s, he began sending envoys to that island nation demanding that its rulers submit to him and pay tribute. But they repeatedly refused, telling him that God was on their side, not his. Intending to force the Japanese into submission, in November 1274

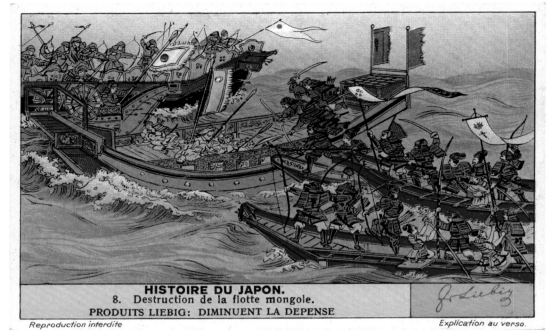

HISTOIRE DU JAPON.
8. Destruction de la flotte mongole.
PRODUITS LIEBIG: DIMINUENT LA DEPENSE

Explication au verso.

Under Kublai Khan, the Mongols attempted to conquer Japan, but their fleet was twice devastated by storms causing the Mongols to withdraw without victory.

the khan launched a large naval force, which crossed from Korea to the Japanese island of Kyushu. Fortunately for the Japanese, a storm hit, capsized many of the ships, and killed 13,200 of the attackers. Kublai Khan assembled an even bigger invasion force—composed of 1,000 vessels and 70,000 Mongols and Koreans—in 1281. Smitha writes,

> For fifty-three days, the Japanese held the invaders to a narrow beachhead on Kyushu. Then a hurricane struck. The Mongols withdrew again, only half of [them] making it back to China. The Japanese interpreted the hurricane as a god-wind—*kamikaze*. Kubilai had found in the Far East the

[territorial] limits that Hulegu had found in the Middle East.[63]

Genghis Khan's Legacy

No Great Khan took Kublai's place after he died in 1294. By that time the various khanates—in China, central Asia, Persia, and Russia—had become independent enough to be regarded as separate kingdoms. These states continued to thrive for a while. But over time they grew weaker, and all collapsed by the mid-1400s. A number of Mongols survived in Mongolia and quietly carried on the old tribal, nomadic ways. Elsewhere in Asia, those who still identified themselves as

Mongols were steadily absorbed into local native populations.

Although the once powerful Mongol Empire was gone, its legacy and that of its founder, the great Genghis Khan, are profound. On the one hand, at their height the Mongols were on the verge of overrunning Europe, an event that would have resulted in a very different world today. On the other hand, mostly because of a coincidence of timing (the unexpected death of Ogedei Khan), the Mongols never managed to conquer Europe. In the long run, that ensured that the European-controlled West would go on to colonize and dominate most of the world for centuries. Scholar Timothy May writes,

> Even today the legacy of Genghis Khan remains impressive. [As] an organizational and strategic genius, [he] created one of the most highly-disciplined and effective armies in history. … Even after he died … Mongol armies dominated the battlefield until the empire stretched from the Pacific Ocean to [the borders of Europe]. His non-military achievements include the introduction of a writing system … still used in Inner

Mongolia today, the idea of religious tolerance throughout the empire, and the achievement of tribal unity among the Mongols. Genghis Khan's greatest accomplishments, however, cannot be counted in terms of territory or victories, but in the presence of a Mongol nation and culture. Mongols today venerate him as the founding father of Mongolia.[64]

Indeed, modern Mongols see the unity the first Great Khan brought long ago to a group of obscure steppe tribes as the very reason for their existence. For that achievement, both they and many other people around the world remember him in a positive light rather than in a negative one as a destroyer. According to one modern expert,

> from Temujin, whose name once evoked derision [scorn], to Genghis Khan, who [awed the peoples of] a fearful outside world, this Mongol emperor is more deserving of fame than of infamy [bad reputation]. He was not only a world conqueror but also a world unifier.[65]

Notes

Introduction: From Barbarian to Modern Man

1. Geoffrey Chaucer, *The Canterbury Tales*, ed. Sinan Kökbugur, Librarius, www.librarius.com/canttran/squitrfs.htm.
2. Jack Weatherford, *Genghis Khan and the Making of the Modern World*. New York: Crown, 2004, p. xviii.
3. Weatherford, *Genghis Khan and the Making of the Modern World*, p. xxxiv.
4. George Lane, *Daily Life in the Mongol Empire*. Westport, CT: Greenwood, 2006, p. 4.
5. Weatherford, *Genghis Khan and the Making of the Modern World*, p. 267.

Chapter One: Ancient Peoples of the Steppes

6. J.J. Saunders, *The History of the Mongol Conquests*. Philadelphia: University of Pennsylvania Press, 2001, p. 44.
7. Lane, *Daily Life in the Mongol Empire*, p. 17.
8. Lane, *Daily Life in the Mongol Empire*, pp. 15–17
9. Quoted in William W. Rockhill, ed. and trans., *The Journey of William of Rubruck to the Eastern Parts of the World, 1953–55*. London: Hakluyt Society, 1900, p. 9.
10. Quoted in Rockhill, *The Journey of William of Rubruck to the Eastern Parts of the World, 1953–55*, p. 9.

11. Quoted in Simon de Saint Quentin, *History of the Tartars*, ed. Jean Richard. Paris: Oriental Library, 1965, p. 40.
12. Peter Brent, *Genghis Khan: The Rise, Authority, and Decline of Mongol Power*. New York: McGraw-Hill, 1976, pp. 29–30.
13. Quoted in Paul Kahn, ed., *The Secret History of the Mongols: The Origin of Chingis Khan*. Boston: Cheng and Tsui, 1998, p. 7.
14. Brent, *Genghis Khan*, p. 30.
15. Giovanni Carpini, *The Story of the Mongols*, in *History of the Mongols* by Bertold Spuler, trans. Helga and Stuart Drummond. London: Routledge and Kegan Paul, 1989, pp. 80–81.
16. Lane, *Daily Life in the Mongol Empire*, p. 184.

Chapter Two: The Rise of Genghis Khan

17. René Grousset, *Conqueror of the World: The Life of Chingis-Khan*. New York: Orion Press, 1966, p. 36.
18. Weatherford, *Genghis Khan and the Making of the Modern World*, pp. xvi–xvii.
19. Kahn, *The Secret History of the Mongols*, p. 13.
20. Kahn, *The Secret History of the Mongols*, pp. 40–41.

21. Quoted in Kahn, *The Secret History of the Mongols*, p. 20.
22. Kahn, *The Secret History of the Mongols*, pp. 21–22.
23. Brent, *Genghis Khan*, p. 16.
24. Minhaj al-Siraj Juzjani, *Tabakat-I-Nasiri: A General History of the Muhammadan Dynasties of Asia*, trans. H.G. Raverty. New Delhi, India: Oriental Books, 1970, p. 1077.
25. Kahn, *The Secret History of the Mongols*, p. 37.
26. Brent, *Genghis Khan*, p. 24.
27. Kahn, *The Secret History of the Mongols*, pp. 111–12.
28. Lane, *Daily Life in the Mongol Empire*, p. 5.

Chapter Three: Military and Legal Reforms

29. Weatherford, *Genghis Khan and the Making of the Modern World*, p. 67.
30. Saunders, *The History of the Mongol Conquests*, p. 52.
31. James Chambers, *The Devil's Horsemen: The Mongol Invasion of Europe*. New York: Book Sales, 2003, p. 54.
32. *Marco Polo,* The Travels of Marco Polo, vol. 1, trans. Henry Yule, Project Gutenberg, January 8, 2004, www.gutenberg.org/files/10636/10636.txt.
33. Polo, *The Travels of Marco Polo*, Project Gutenberg.
34. Chambers, *The Devil's Horsemen*, pp. 59–60.
35. Marco Polo, *The Travels of Marco Polo*. New York: Orion Press, pp. 113–14.
36. Polo, *The Travels of Marco Polo*, Project Gutenberg.
37. John R. Elting, *The Super-Strategists: Great Captains, Theorists, and Fighting Men Who Have Shaped the History of Warfare*. New York: Scribner's, 1989, pp. 227–28.
38. Per Inge Oestmoen, "The Mongol Military Might," The Realm of the Mongols (Web site), www.coldsiberia.org/monmight.htm.
39. Quoted in Elting, *The Super-Strategists*, pp. 238–39.
40. Ata-Malik Juvaini, *History of the World-Conqueror*, vol. 1, trans. John A. Boyle. England: Manchester University Press, 1958, p. 204. www.archive.org/stream/historyofthewor1011691mbp/historyofthewor1011691mbp_djvu.txt.
41. Frank E. Smitha, "Genghis Khan and the Great Mongol Empire," Macrohistory and World Report (Web site), www.fsmitha.com/h3/h11mon.htm.

Chapter Four: Subduing Northern China

42. China National Tourist Office, "Welcome to the Silk Road," China National Tourist Office, www.cnto.org/silkroad.asp.
43. Kahn, *The Secret History of the Mongols*, pp. 148–49.
44. Brent, *Genghis Khan*, p. 48.
45. Kahn, *The Secret History of the Mongols*, p. 147.
46. Kahn, *The Secret History of the Mongols*, p. 148.
47. Weatherford, *Genghis Khan and the Making of the Modern World*, p. 101.
48. Saunders, *The History of the Mongol Conquests*, p. 68.
49. Quoted in E. Bretschneider, *Medieval Researches from Eastern Asiatic Sources*, vol. 1. New York: Barnes and Noble, 1967, pp. 37–39.

Chapter Five: Conquests in Western Asia

50. Quoted in Juzjani, *Tabakat-I-Nasiri*, p. 966.
51. Juvaini, *History of the World-Conqueror*, p. 80.
52. Juvaini, *History of the World-Conqueror*, p. 80
53. Saunders, *The History of the Mongol Conquests*, p. 56.
54. Quoted in al-Siraj Juzjani, *Tabakat-I-Nasiri*, p. 105.
55. Edward Gibbon, *The Decline and Fall of the Roman Empire*, vol. 3, ed. David Womersley. New York: Penguin, 1994, p. 797.
56. Gibbon, *The Decline and Fall of the Roman Empire*, p. 798.
57. Saunders, *The History of the Mongol Conquests*, p. 59.
58. Weatherford, *Genghis Khan and the Making of the Modern World*, p. 119.
59. Saunders, *The History of the Mongol Conquests*, p. 69.
60. Kahn, *The Secret History of the Mongols*, p. 165.

Chapter Six: The Mongols After Genghis Khan

61. John France, "Liegnitz," in *The Seventy Great Battles in History*, by Jeremy Black, ed. London: Thames and Hudson, 2005, p. 67.
62. Frank E. Smitha, "Mongols to the Gates of Vienna," Macrohistory and World Report (Web site), www.fsmitha.com/h3/mongols02.htm.
63. Frank E. Smitha, "Kublai Khan in China and to Japan," Macrohistory and World Report (Web site), www.fsmitha.com/h3/mongols04.htm.
64. Timothy May, "Genghis Khan (1165–1227)," San Antonio College, www.alamo.edu/sac/history/keller/mongols/empsub1.html.
65. Lane, *Daily Life in the Mongol Empire*, p. 2.

Glossary

anda: A blood brother.

arban: A Mongol army unit containing ten men.

ballista: A giant crossbow.

batur: A Mongol clan leader.

capital offense: A crime punishable by death.

captargac: A leather bag used to carry bones and other items.

cavalry: Mounted soldiers.

codify: To set down in writing.

composite bow: A very powerful bow made by gluing together pieces of wood, animal horn, and sinew.

dowry: Money or other valuables given by a bride's father to her husband for the upkeep of the marriage.

dynasty: A family line of rulers.

effigies (ongghot): Small statues representing spirits.

exogamy: A custom in which a person married someone from a different tribe.

felt: Compressed wool.

ger (or yurt): A tentlike house that could be easily assembled and dismantled.

gurkhan: Among the Mongols, a chief elder.

Great Yasa: The law code established by Genghis Khan between 1206 and 1218.

infantry: Foot soldiers.

intelligence (military): Useful information about the enemy.

irgen: A Mongol tribe.

jagun: A Mongol army unit containing a hundred men.

kam: A Mongol shaman.

khanate: A separate, regional Mongol realm.

koumiss: An alcoholic drink made by fermenting mare's milk.

kuriltai: A big meeting or council.

lance: A spear used by a mounted horsemen to poke or stab his opponents.

mercenaries: Paid soldiers.

minghan: A Mongol army unit containing a thousand men.

noyan: High-ranking Mongol military officers.

obok: A Mongol clan, composed of several families.

pastoral nomads: People who raise animals for a living and move from place to place to feed and maintain them.

regent: An adult who temporarily rules in place of a minor until the latter is old enough to assume leadership.

shaman: A spirit guide or medicine man thought to possess the ability to interpret the will of various spirits or gods.

shamanism: A belief in nature spirits and/or the spirits of ancestors.

stealth warfare: The use of tactics designed to fool the enemy.

steppe: A mostly flat, often grassy plain.

trebuchet: A large, catapult-like siege device that could hurl rocks long distances.

tribute: Money or valuables paid to acknowledge one's submission.

tumen: A Mongol army unit containing ten thousand men.

vassal: A follower or dependent puppet ruler.

yasa: Mongol laws or justice.

Yeke Mongol Ulus: The Mongol nation created by Genghis Khan.

For More Information

Books

Christon I. Archer et al., *World History of Warfare*. Lincoln: University of Nebraska Press, 2002. This book provides an excellent overview of the evolution of warfare across the globe.

Peter Brent, *Genghis Khan: The Rise, Authority, and Decline of Mongol Power*. New York: McGraw-Hill, 1976. This is a well-researched study of the Mongol Empire.

James Chambers, *The Devil's Horsemen: The Mongol Invasion of Europe*. New York: Book Sales, 2003. Now seen as a classic of its kind, this book cites all of the known European sources about the Mongol invasion.

William Honeychurch et al., *Genghis Khan and the Mongol Empire*. Ulaanbaatar, Mongolia: Genghis Khan Exhibits, 2009. This is a beautifully mounted volume written by a series of noted scholars.

Peter Jackson, *The Mongols and the West, 1221–1410*. London: Longman, 2005. This is an excellent source of information by a major authority on Mongols.

Paul Kahn, ed., *The Secret History of the Mongols: The Origin of Chingis Khan*. Boston: Cheng and Tsui, 1998. This book is an adaptation of a fine translation by Francis Woodman Cleaves of the famous primary source about Genghis Khan and his heirs.

George Lane, *Daily Life in the Mongol Empire*. Westport, CT: Greenwood, 2006. This is the best available modern source on Mongol society and customs.

Paul Lococo, *Genghis Khan: History's Greatest Empire Builder*. Washington, DC: Potomac, 2008. This synopsis of the subject is well researched and very well written.

John Man, *Genghis Khan: Life, Death and Resurrection*. New York: St. Martin's, 2007. Man provides a thoughtful overview of the life of the famous Mongol conqueror.

Paul Ratchnevsky, *Genghis Khan: His Life and Legacy*. Oxford, UK: Blackwell, 1993. One of the leading authorities on the Mongols delivers an informative study of Genghis Khan.

J.J. Saunders, *The History of the Mongol Conquests*. Philadelphia: University of Pennsylvania Press, 2001. This book provides useful details about various Mongol battles, campaigns, and policies.

S.R. Turnbull, *Genghis Khan and the Mongol Conquests*. Oxford, UK: Osprey, 2003. This is a concise, well-researched overview of the many wars waged by the founder of the Mongol Empire.

S.R. Turnbull, *Mongol Warrior, 1200–1350*. Oxford, UK: Osprey, 2003. This book contains large amounts of information about the Mongol army and the weapons it used.

Jack Weatherford, *Genghis Khan and the Making of the Modern World*. New York: Crown, 2004. A thorough and well-written book on Genghis Khan.

Internet Sources

Los Angeles County Museum of Art, "Map of the Mongol Empire," Los Angeles County Museum of Art, 2003, www. lacma.org/khan/map.htm.

Per Inge Oestmoen, "The Mongolian Bow," The Realm of the Mongols, www. coldsiberia.org/monbow.htm.

Per Inge Oestmoen, "Women in Mongol Society," The Realm of the Mongols, www.coldsiberia.org/monwomen. htm.

Per Inge Oestmoen, "The Yasa of Chingis Khan: A Code of Honor, Dignity, and Excellence," The Realm of the Mongols, www.coldsiberia.org/ webdoc9.htm.

Silk Road Foundation, "Marco Polo and His Travels," Silk Road Foundation, www.silk-road.com/artl/marco-polo.shtml.

Web Site

The Mongols (http://members.tripod. com/~whitebard/ca54.htm). Contains informative articles about the Mongols and their society.

Index

A

Abaqa, 80
Accomplishments and legacy of
    Genghis Khan, 11, 82–83
Administrative reforms, 71–72
Ancestral spirits, 26
Archery, 43–46, *44, 45*
Ariq Buqa, 80
Army. *See* Military
Assassins, 78–79

B

Baghdad, 78–79
Batu, 76, 77, 78
Bekhter, 30
Blood brotherhood, 30
    See also Jamuka
Borte, 29, 32, 34
Bows (weapons), 43–46, *44, 45*
Bukhara, 69, *70*
Burkhan Khan, 56–57, 73

C

The Canterbury Tales (Chaucer), 9–10
Capital punishment, 50
Captivity of Genghis Khan, 31–32
Catapults, 60, *60,* 61
Chagatai, 52, 73
Chaucer, Geoffrey, 9–10
Childhood of Genghis Khan, 27–32
Clans, 18
Climate, 14–15, *15*
Clothing, 21, *22,* 41
Conquests. *See* Warfare and conquest

D

Dading, 59
Death of Genghis Khan, 73–74, *74*
Death penalty, 50

E

Eastern Europe, 75–77
Economic reforms, 71–72
Effigies, 26
Europe, 75–77, *77,* 83

F

Family
    childhood of Genghis Khan, 29–31
    Mongols, 17–19
    sons, 52, *53*
    succession, 72–73, 77–78, 80
Food and drink, 21, 22

G

Genghis Khan, 8–13, *11, 27, 30, 33,*
    66, 74
    accomplishments and legacy, 11,
        82–83
    captivity, 31–32
    Chaucer's version of, 9–10
    childhood, 27–32
    death of, 73–74
    economic and administrative
        reforms, 71–72
    Khwarizm, conquest of, 67–70
    legal reform, 48–51
    maintaining unity, 39
    military organization, 40–42

Muhammad II, peace agreement
   with, 65–67
religious tolerance, 63–64
shamans, influence of, 26
sons of, 52
Geography, 14–15
Great Hunt, 42–43
Great Yasa, 48
Guyuk, 77–78

H
Henry II, Duke, 76
Hoelun, 29, 30
Horses, 22–23, 23, 24–25, 46, 47
Housing, 19, 19–21, 20
Hulegu, 78, 78–79, 80

J
Jamuka, 30, 36–37
Japan, 81–82, 82
Jebe, 68, 70, 71
Jochi, 52, 53, 73
Jurched, 58–59, 61–62
Justice system, 48–51

K
Khan, title of, 36
Khwarizm, 65–70, 68
Kidnapping of Borte, 34
Koumiss, 21, 22
Kublai Khan, 79–82, 80

L
Language, 48
Laws. See Great Yasa
Lifestyle of the Mongols, 15, 15–17,
   62–63

M
Maps
   Mongol Empire, 9, 76
   Mongolia, present day, 10

Silk Road, 55
Marriage, 18, 23–24, 32, 34
Merkid, 34
Mesopotamia, 78–79
Metal technology, 17
Middle East, 79
Military, 40
   discipline and training, 42–43
   horsemanship, 46
   organizational reform, 40–42
   protective gear, 41
   weapons, 43, 43–46, 44, 45
   See also Warfare and conquest
Mongke, 78, 78, 80
Mongolia
   climate and geography, 14–15, 15
   present day, 10
   thirteenth century, 9
Mongols, 8–12
   clothing, 21, 22
   conquest of rival tribes, 34–37
   food and drink, 21, 22
   horses, 23
   housing, 19, 19–21, 20
   legacy of Genghis Khan, 82–83
   nomadism, 15–17
   tribes and family, 17–19
   unity among tribes, 37–38
   wealthy lifestyle, 62–63
   women's roles, 23–25, 24
Muhammad II, 65–67, 70

N
Nomadism, 15, 15–17
Northern China
   Jurched, 58–59, 61–62
   Mongols, rivalry with the, 17
   Tangut, 55–57, 57, 73, 73–74

O
Ogedei, 52, 53, 73, 75–77, 79
Ong Khan, 34, 37

P
Persia, 78–79
Polo, Marco, 48, 80, *80*, 81
Punishment, 50–51

R
Reconstruction and rebuilding, 69
Reform
    defeated opponents, treatment of, 36
    economic and administrative, 71–72
    laws and justice, 48–51
    military, 39–43
Religion, 25–26, 63–64
Rescue of Borte, 34
Russia, 11, 75

S
Samarkand, 69
Senggum, 37
Shamanism, 25–26
Siege warfare, 60, 61
Silk Road, *55*, 55–56
Sorkhan, 32
Southern China, 81
Soviet Union, former, 12
Spirituality, 25–26
Stealth warfare, 47
Steppes, 14–15
Subodei, 70, 75, 76
Succession, 72–73, 77–78, 80

T
Tangut, 55–57, *57*, 73, 73–74
Targutai, 31
Tayichiguds, 31–32
Technology
    catapults, 60, *60*, 61
    innovation exchange, 56
    metal, 17
    weapons, 43–44

Title of khan, 36
Tools, 17
Trade routes, 56, 65
Transportation, 21, 22–23, *23*
Tribes, 17–19, 34–38
Tuli, 52, 73

W
Warfare and conquest, *16*, *35*, *58*
    battlefield tactics, 46–48, 58–59, 61
    catapults, use of, 60, *60*
    Europe, 75–77, *77*
    historic image of the Mongols, 11–12
    Japan, 81–82, *82*
    Jurched, 58–59, 61–62
    Khwarizm, 67–70
    Middle East, 78–79
    nomadic lifestyle, 16–17
    Southern China, 81
    Tangut, 55–57, *57*, 73, 73–74
    Western Asia, 67–70
    See also Military
Wealth, 62–63
Weapons
    bows, *43*, 43–46, *44*, 45
    catapults, 60, *60*, 61
    technology, 17
Western Asia, 65–70
Women's roles, 23–25, *24*
Writing system, 48

X
Xuanzong, 58–59, 61–62

Y
Yesugei, 29
Yurts, *19*, 19–21, *20*

Picture Credits

About the Author

In addition to his acclaimed volumes on the ancient world, historian Don Nardo has produced several studies of medieval times, including *Life on a Medieval Pilgrimage*, *The Italian Renaissance*, *The Inquisition*, *The Vikings*, and a biography of medieval astronomer Tycho Brahe. He has also produced volumes about medieval warfare, the King Arthur legends, and the age of exploration. Nardo resides with his wife, Christine, in Massachusetts.